"Dr. Coller brings out a well-balanced mixture of medicine and the Word of God. As a doctor, he shows how the use of medicine and faith in the Word of God work together. This book points out principles that are important to understand for a healthy body and soul. Dr. Coller has a great love for the Lord as well as His people. His heart is to see everyone healthy—both spiritually *and* physically. Thank you, Dr. Coller, for the time, effort, and knowledge you put into this wonderful book."

—Edward J Lixey,
Jehu Ministries International

revelations
in a brown paper bag

Dr. Gary H. Coller

revelations
in a brown paper bag

*Divine Health and
Wisdom Based Fundamentals
of Health and Healing*

TATE PUBLISHING
AND ENTERPRISES, LLC

Revelations in a Brown Paper Bag
Copyright © 2012 by Dr. Gary H. Coller. All rights reserved.

No part of this publication may be reproduced, stored in a retrieval system or transmitted in any way by any means, electronic, mechanical, photocopy, recording or otherwise without the prior permission of the author except as provided by USA copyright law.

Scripture quotations marked (AMP) are taken from the *Amplified Bible*, Copyright © 1954, 1958, 1962, 1964, 1965, 1987 by The Lockman Foundation. Used by permission.

Scripture quotations marked (ESV) are from *The Holy Bible, English Standard Version*®, copyright © 2001 by Crossway Bibles, a publishing ministry of Good News Publishers. Used by permission. All rights reserved.

Scripture quotations marked (KJV) are taken from the *Holy Bible, King James Version*®, Cambridge, 1769. Used by permission. All rights reserved.

Scripture quotations marked (NIV) are taken from the *Holy Bible, New International Version*®, Copyright © 1973, 1978, 1984 by International Bible Society. Used by permission of Zondervan Publishing House. All rights reserved.

Scripture quotations marked (NLT) are taken from the *Holy Bible, New Living Translation*, copyright © 1996. Used by permission of Tyndale House Publishers, Inc., Wheaton, Illinois 60189. All rights reserved.

Scripture quotations marked (NASB) are taken from the *New American Standard Bible*®, Copyright © 1960, 1962, 1963, 1968, 1971, 1972, 1973, 1975, 1977, 1995 by The Lockman Foundation. Used by permission.

Scripture quotations marked (lamsa) are from the *Holy Bible from Ancient Eastern Manuscripts*, copyright © 1933, 1939, 1940, 1957, 1961, 1967, 1968 by A.J. Holman Co.

This book is designed to provide accurate and authoritative information with regard to the subject matter covered. This information is given with the understanding that neither the author nor Tate Publishing, LLC is engaged in rendering legal, professional advice. Since the details of your situation are fact dependent, you should additionally seek the services of a competent professional.

The opinions expressed by the author are not necessarily those of Tate Publishing, LLC.

Published by Tate Publishing & Enterprises, LLC
127 E. Trade Center Terrace | Mustang, Oklahoma 73064 USA
1.888.361.9473 | www.tatepublishing.com

Tate Publishing is committed to excellence in the publishing industry. The company reflects the philosophy established by the founders, based on Psalm 68:11,
"The Lord gave the word and great was the company of those who published it."

Book design copyright © 2012 by Tate Publishing, LLC. All rights reserved.
Cover design by Joel Uber
Interior design by Lindsay B. Behrens

Published in the United States of America
ISBN: 978-1-61862-950-0
1. Religion / Christian Life / Spiritual Growth
2. Health & Fitness / General
12.04.09

Author's Note

On July 2, 2002 I received a prophetic word that the Lord was putting a book in me that would bless many people. Over the next couple of years many attempts were made to start the book. The attempts proved fruitless. I gave up my efforts to even start a book for more than a year. Then one morning a patient presented to my office and said, "I don't know why I am here." I replied, "Neither do I." To which she responded, "When I woke up this morning God told me to come in and see you, Dr. Coller. I think I am supposed to pray with you." She went on, "Do you pray in tongues?" I acknowledged that I usually limit that sort of thing to my 'closet time with God'; so she asked if I interpret tongues. I replied, "no." Obviously, I was not making this easy for her. Despite that she continued in obedience to God and began to pray for me...in tongues. After a short time of prayer she stopped and she looked at me and said, "God told you to write a book and he wants it done!"

Shortly after this encounter I began waking up in the middle of the night with what I called revelations. I suddenly had insights illuminating certain scriptures. I would write down those revelations and throw the papers into a brown paper bag. Thus, the title, Revelations in a Brown Paper Bag aka Divine Health-Wisdom Based Fundamentals of Health and Healing.

—Dr. Gary H. Coller

Foreword

"Let me hear in the morning of your steadfast love, for in you I trust. Make me know the way I should go, for to you I lift up my soul" (Psalms 143:8, ESV).

"In the morning the Word of the LORD came to me" (Ezekiel 12:8, ESV).

Much of what we have received in direction, leading, and destiny is given to us by the Lord in what is called the "spirit time of the day." It is when the Creator of all heavens speaks to us in order to give us the dreams, visions, and leading of instruction that will help us to walk out the destiny of what He has intended for us to do from the time of our being in the womb of our mother (Psalm 139:13-18).

As we come into acknowledging that our God can and will speak to us in order to set our paths of life into His perfect will, His covenant is made very obvious to us by how He sends the Holy Ghost to not only abide in us but to lead us in all truth. As you and I pursue this open door of a Loving Father in order to know what He has for us, it becomes easier to not only hear His voice but to go deeper in knowing His perfect will for each of us.

As you look through the Bible, you discover that many times the Lord would come to a person through the early dawning of the day in order to give them His Word for His people. This is how it was with the prophets of the Old Testament, and in this early rising, there came an understanding that as the prophet pursued the revelation of what God was giving, there came a benefit to give the people the hope of being in relationship with Him.

Many times, the saints will request of the Lord to speak to them, and while it may not be comfortable, it is a necessary act of obedience and love that will open the door of fellowship with God the Father through His Son and our Redeemer Jesus Christ. Now, when we make a written record of these times of awakening, instruction, and acknowledging an open door for being trained by Him, we are also establishing a protocol of Holy Ghost to give to others. In this giving of the report of the Lord to others, what we are truly doing is making Matthew 28:19 come into reality. "Go therefore and make disciples of all nations, baptizing them in the name of the Father and of the Son and of the Holy Spirit."

It is in this equipping of training the church to become disciples that we not only cause increase in numbers, but we also provide training that will help others to do the ministry of the saints (Ephesians 4:11-12).

As you read this book and glean the revelation that has been given by the Lord, you will see the heart of a servant who is willing to give all that he has in order to have more of the Lord in his life. You and I will discover that this book is about being willing to go so far in life as to prefer others and to serve the saints in order to bring their identity of Christ in them the hope of glory to a reality (Colossians 1:27). And then, as this realization comes, we can see that in the willingness to seek God first, there is no holding back by the Lord of hosts to let His people know that He has the desire to be involved in each of our lives on a personal level.

It is a joy when we not only hear the Lord, but we also know that He is so in love with us that He would take time to stir us awake to receive instruction in order to provide even answers to others who may be seeking the leading of His Spirit. In the reading of this book, you will discover what can be called "early morning revelations for everyday living." In some of it, we can chuckle and smile knowing that what we are reading is not only for author, but for us as well, for we are all one body, and it is quite evident here.

And as you read, watch as the Lord will see your interest and then awaken you, too, to receive even more of the nuggets of wisdom and understanding that would shape new lives and new hopes.

In Jesus Christ's Name!

—Pat Holloran,
Harvest House International Ministries

Table of Contents

Introduction 17
   Finding Truth in an Empty Cup 17

No Hands but Ours 21

Personal Testimony: "The Wine Press Sucks…
So Praise God!" 23

Spiritual Foundations 29
   Introduction 29
   Faith in the Goodness of God 35
   In Opposition to God, Satan Hates Mankind 37
   The Fruits of the Trees in the Garden 39
   Tree of Life 44
   Tree of the Knowledge of Good and Evil 47
   The God-Centered Life 51

The Structure of Man 63
Love Meter 67

Soul Power 69
  Life Energy 69
  External Energy Sources 72
  Internal Energy Sources 79

Seven Deadly Sins 91
  Seven Things the Lord Hates 94

Healing Scriptures 97
  Build Your Faith, Overcome Your Fears 99
  You Have Authority in Christ—Resist Fear! 104
  You Are An Overcomer! 106
  Jesus is Lord so Close All Doors to the Enemy! 108
  God's Word Brings Healing! 110
  Healing Is a Good Gift from God! 113
  We Have Been Redeemed from the Bondage of Sickness and Disease! 114
  Snap Out of that Depression—Your Attitude Determines Your Altitude! 115
  Have Confidence in Him—God Cannot Lie! 116
  Base Your Faith on God's Promises—Long Life Belongs to You! 117
  Your Words are Important and Powerful! 118

Listen to Jesus...Not Your Body! 119
Give Testimony of Your Healing! 119
Hold On to Your Healing! 120

Building Faith................................... 123
  Overcome Doubt............................... 123
  Fasting 125
  Speak God's Truth.............................. 128

Natural Aging 133
  The Mighty River of God......................... 133
  Some Important Functional Medicine Concepts 140

Worldly Influences on Health and Healing 159
  Dependence on Prescription Drugs.................. 159
  Medical Theory—Germ Theory versus Biological Terrain 161
  Chemicals and Disease 165

The Web of Functional Health 175

Practical Advice for Living a Long, Healthy Life 179
  The Basics 179
  Eating Habits and General Nutritional Advise 181
  Personality Issues 182
  Your Support Structure 184

Crossing Over..187
  Keys to the Kingdom..........................187
  A Thought for the Terminally Ill................190
  Last Thoughts................................191

Endnotes...193

Introduction

Finding Truth in an Empty Cup
If you desire revelation of truth, you must start with an empty cup. That is, you must rid yourself of all preconceived notions. Scripture says that wisdom begins with the fear of God. An empty cup with the fear of God is the foundation of truth. Contemplate all you encounter from that prospective.

Pride, politics, economy, the cares of this world, etc. all fill our cup with half truths and overt falsehoods that protect our selfish interests. Such self-serving conclusions dilute truth and block revelation. If we do not focus on eliminating personal biases, we fall into a state of relative truths and humanism. We then find ourselves in a position of forever attempting to reconcile new data into a contradicting belief system.

"Evolution" is an example. Evolution is considered truth because a majority of people believe it. It is what is taught in school. There was even a famous court case that confirmed the science of evolution over creation. Despite this, the basic scientific support for evolution is lacking. If we evolved from slime, where are the transitional organisms? I am told that, genetically, the closest animal to a human is a pig. Furthermore, a basic law of physics is that entropy increases. Nature moves from a state of order to disorder. It requires energy to hold things together. As the energy holding things together depletes, the things fall apart. Things naturally move from more complex to less complex. Does this mean, if evolution is a scientific reality, that people are evolving *into* pigs?…Just a thought.

So start with no preconceived notions and allow yourself to be open to God's truth. As you read this book, there may be parts that you find hard to accept. Please continue reading. Just like when we, as new believers in Christ, get hung up on seeming contradictions in scripture, if we continue in faith, those "contradictions" vanish as we learn more and as God illuminates His truth to us.

Please understand that this book is written to express fundamentals of health and healing from the God-centered (in Christ) perspective. Individual concepts, such as the "fruits" expressed in a person's life (both positive and negative) may be cultivated in other ways. We can learn behavioral principals outside of God. They may be established by such things as governmental laws, influence and discipline from family, peer group pressure, or personal conviction. In other words, God's laws can be learned outside the framework of faith. In our culture, societal, familial, and personal mandates are often founded on Judeo Christian principles.

Just as what we say and do influences the world around us, the influence of the world can strongly affect our beliefs, and the fruits manifest in our lives. Perhaps that is why people who believe they are inherently good may find no reason to accept Christ. Those of us that accept that we mess up time after time know our need for Christ. We can then plug into God's truths as they are illuminated through His Word.

It is then our responsibility to act on what we have learned.

Knowledge is knowing what to do…Wisdom is doing it.

No Hands but Ours

Shortly after the end of the Second World War, a quaint little French village was bombed by mistake. In the old city square, a large statue of Jesus Christ had stood with His hands outspread in an attitude of invitation. On the pedestal was the phrase "Come Unto Me."

When the figure was being reassembled, all of the pieces, except for the hands, were found in the rubble. When the hands could not be found, someone suggested that new hands be made.

But the people protested, "No—leave Him without hands!"

So today, in the public square, the restored statue of Christ stands without hands. Now the words on its base read, "Christ Has No Hands—No Hands but Ours." [1]

This point applies to health and healing and is emphasized in the biblical passage…

"He who is loose or slack in his work is brother to him who is a destroyer [and he who does not use his endeavor to heal himself is brother to him who commits suicide]" Proverbs 18:9, (AMP).

Personal Testimony: "The Wine Press Sucks... So Praise God!"

There I was…a young grape—plump, juicy, and ripe with life. By my junior year of high school, I was president of my class. I had a girlfriend and plenty of friends. I thought I had it all. That was the perspective of a young, ripe grape that was very full of himself and the world. Little did I know that the owner's manual for grapes, the Holy Bible, spoke of new wineskins and new wine. It even says that you can't put new wine in "old wine skins." God had to break the old wine skin of my self-centered life to fill me with the new wine of a God-centered life. Let me tell you, being broken is not fun. As my friend and mentor in the Lord, Ed Lixey, loves to say, "The wine press sucks."

When I first started the God-centered walk, I ran into tremendous opposition. It was 1978. I was a young intern. I was laughed at and ridiculed as being weak because I needed a God. I couldn't handle life on my own. These allegations were coming from people who seemed to believe they were gods in their own right. As a young doctor working in a hospital, I was not in a position to defend myself. An intern can be much like the proverbial dog you might kick when frustrated. I had to take it or possibly lose my chances to fulfill the requirements to practice medicine on my own… my life dream.

I was working twelve out of every fourteen days doing twelve hour shifts. I would also be called into the hospital in the middle of the night for "interesting cases" or to deliver babies. I was tired, stressed, and harassed. At the hospital, there was a definite line drawn between Christian and non-Christian doctors. I had the support of the Christians and the chastisement of the others. Some went so far as to lie about my actions. One doctor hid my board exams in the bottom of a drawer in his office, rather than send them in for my certification. Luckily, they were found by a Christian secretary who sent them in for me. A spiritual battle was raging. I could do little but pray and do what was asked of me.

Soon, though, I developed severe headaches. Doctors would say, "It's probably just the stress." After months of pain, a doctor ordered x-rays of my head, and a tumor was discovered. To make matters worse, a patient at the hospital with the same condition had just died!

I began my search to find the best qualified doctor to help me. I went to doctors all over the state, but back in 1978, I could not find anyone that had even scrubbed the surgery I required, let alone someone that had actually performed it successfully.

God is great, though. I attended a seminar at Cleveland Clinic, and the doctor lecturing turned out to be the world authority on my condition. He had a great deal of experience—and success! I spoke with him. He took x-rays. He then said, "Go home and get your will in order. This is serious. Come back next week for surgery."

I did exactly as I was told. But when I got home, I called a friend and mentor of mine.

You see, when I was in osteopathic training, I helped develop a Christian coffee house in Lansing called "The Master's House." It was an alternative to going to bars. We had Christian rock and roll, served Kool-Aid and popcorn, and had fellowship.

The elders at "The Master's House" were Dick and Muriel Welsh. They had an incredible anointing. It was Dick that I called with my medical concerns. He assured me that everything would be okay and that he would pray.

A couple of nights later, they visited me at my townhouse. We briefly discussed my situation, and they quickly took it to the Lord. They anointed me with oil and prayed. I remember that they focused on the fact that God forgave me of anything I had ever done and that He loved me.

I soon experienced a tingling in my feet. The tingling increased in intensity as it slowly began to move up my body. It picked up more speed and intensity as it moved toward my head. Then, suddenly, it felt like fifty pounds had been lifted off my shoulders, neck, and my head! I began to weep. "What do I do now?" I asked.

Dick responded confidently, "Never limit the way God will heal. Go back to Cleveland and see what the doctors say. Follow their advice."

I went back to Cleveland Clinic, and the doctor took more x-rays. The tumor was gone!

What a high place I was at with Jesus. You would think that after an experience like that, Satan would have no inroads. I should ride out the rest of my life in victory after victory, stomping on Satan's head.

Well, no. I came back to my internship where I suffered continual harassment, even threats to disqualify my internship because I missed time due to my medical condition. I was forced to extend the internship to make up for lost time. Despite all that I went through though, I was finally done.

That was just one year of the wine press. Because I was what you might refer to as a stubborn grape, I did not want to give up my old wineskin easily. In God's love, I had many more years of pressure to break me so that God could truly reside in me to guide me and let His love shine through me. I have come a long way, but as it does for everyone, life requires a daily battle to resist Satan so he will flee. It is a daily battle to resist self-centered inclinations and decide for God.

Now that I have been a practicing physician for nearly thirty years, with a lovely wife and six children, all of which love the Lord, I look back on those times of trial and realize that God never forsook me. He was always there in his perfect timing. What a great and wonderful God we serve!

Key to health—Accepting the fact that, in Christ, you are forgiven, and God considers you worthy.

"For God so loved the world that He even gave His only begotten Son, so that whoever believes in Him should not perish, but have eternal life" John 3:16, (Lamsa).

Spiritual Foundations

Introduction

By way of introduction, my name is Dr. Gary Coller. I am an ordained pastor, an assistant clinical professor in the College of Osteopathic Medicine at Michigan State University, and an Osteopathic Physician Board Certified in Family Practice and Clinical Metal Toxicology. I am also certified in Advanced Integrative Medicine.

I have been practicing what is now called "functional medicine" since the early 1980s. That makes me one of the most experienced doctors practicing functional medicine in the United States. I say that not to impress anyone but to rather establish my credentials for writing this book. My proudest accomplishment is the fact that I have been attending the school of the Holy Ghost for decades.

I acknowledge His guidance in my life and in the writing of this book.

It is that guidance that led me to the realization that with experience comes responsibility. This book is written to share a healing paradigm that is understood by few physicians. The lack of understanding is because medical training, with few exceptions, addresses disease by attacking disease symptoms with drugs and surgery. Medicine, in large part, has ignored basic functional issues that result in disease. This book is devoted to opening doctors' eyes to truths and to giving patients hope for the cures for disease by focusing on the causes of the disease more than the symptoms of the disease.

To that effect, I want to acknowledge the existence of our entire being—spirit, soul, and body. I will then address each component and how each relates to disease, health, and healing.

It has been said that medical knowledge more than doubles every four years. With that, there have been studies done that confirm such things as the power of prayer, the power of the spoken word, and the value of fasting. Yet much of the church lives in fear of acknowledging these and other truths established by God's Word in the Bible.

"But know this, that in the last days perilous times will come: for men will be lovers of themselves, lovers of money, boasters, proud, blasphemers, disobedient to parents, unthankful, unholy, unloving, unforgiving, slanderers, without self control, brutal, despisers of good, traitors, headstrong, haughty, lovers of pleasure rather than lovers of God, having a form of Godliness but denying its power. And from such people turn away!" 2 Timothy 3:1-5 (NKJV)

In the great commission in Matthew 28:18-20 (KJV), Jesus said,

"All power is given unto me in heaven and in earth. Go ye therefore, and teach all nations, baptizing them in the name of the Father, and of the Son, and of the Holy Ghost. Teaching them to observe all things whatsoever I have commanded you: And lo I am with you always, even unto the end of the world."

In Mark 16:17-18 (KJV) Jesus said,

"And these signs shall follow them that believe. In my name they shall cast out devils; they shall speak with new tongues; they shall take up serpents; and if they drink any deadly thing, it shall not hurt them; they shall lay hands on the sick, and they shall recover."

If we believe His Word, we will see the glory of God. As we let Jesus become the center of our lives, we become the vessels of His glory. His promises will be manifested through us. We will be blessed to be a blessing to others. Acts 5:16 (NKJV) says, "Also a multitude gathered from the surrounding cities to Jerusalem bringing sick people and those who were tormented by unclean spirits and they were all healed." Even after Jesus had been crucified, we see Jesus working through his disciples to heal. Hebrews 13:8 (NKJV) verifies that Jesus is the same yesterday, today, and forever. Malachi 3:6 (NKJV) says, "For I am the Lord, I do not change." As Christ is centered into our lives, He works through us to accomplish His will.

Some say that the healing stopped with the apostles. To believe this would be denying the Word of God. It would be denying the experience of Paul and of Stephen in the Bible, and it would require a person to ignore the experiences of many all over the world. For example, the book *Megashift* by James Rutz documents that in areas of the world where people stand on their child-like faith, healings are occurring on a regular basis.[2] God manifests in an environment of faith. The church can no longer afford to be anemic. The scriptures tell us that Paul did not persuade people to follow Christ with his eloquence but rather by demonstrating the power of the kingdom. We should follow Paul's example.

To that end, we will start our journey looking at the consequences of a self-centered existence versus a God-centered existence. We will discuss the emotions that follow our choice and the fruits of these emotions. We will see how turning back to a God-centered life heals negative emotions, and physical healings follow. We will then discuss faith and the scriptural healing paradigm based on the shed blood of Jesus. By His stripes, we were healed. We will help you build your faith with scripture. Faith comes by hearing the Word of God (Romans 10:17, Lamsa). We will then look at fasting as a means to more clearly focusing spiritually and as a means of detoxifying your body. We will then transition into basic functional medicine to better understand the body, how it works, and how outside forces cause disease. You will not be left hanging! We will give you action points, spell out keys to health, provide reading assignments and resources to help you reach and maintain optimal health for you and those you encounter.

Key to health—Belief

> When the Sabbath came, He began to teach in the synagogue, and many who heard Him were astonished, and said, Whence did He receive all this? And what wisdom is this which is given to him that wonders like these are wrought by his hands? Is He not the carpenter, the son of Mary, and the brother of James and Joses and Judas and Simon? And behold, are not His sisters here with us? And they denounced Him. And Jesus said to them, there is no prophet who is belittled, except in his own city and among his own brothers and in his own house. And He could not perform a single miracle there, except that He laid His hand on a few sick people and healed them. And He wondered at their lack of faith. And He traveled in the villages teaching.
>
> Mark 6:2-6, (Lamsa)

Faith in the Goodness of God

Fundamental to the God-centered approach to health and healing is that God is absolute goodness. To that end, I would like to share an e-mail correspondence I received. The author was anonymous.

"Did God create everything that exists? Does evil exist? Did God create evil?"

A university professor at a well known institution of higher learning challenged his students with this question. "Did God create everything that exists?"

A student bravely replied, "Yes, He did!"

"God created *everything*?" the professor asked.

"Yes, sir, he certainly did," the student replied.

The professor answered, "If God created everything, then God created evil. And, since evil exists, and according to the principal that our works define who we are, then we can assume God is evil."

The student became quiet and did not respond to the professor's hypothetical definition. The professor, quite pleased with himself, boasted to the students that he had proven once more that the Christian faith was a myth.

Another student raised his hand and said, "May I ask you a question, professor?"

"Of course," the professor replied.

The student stood up and asked, "Professor, does cold exist?"

"What kind of question is this? Of course it exists. Have you never been cold?"

The students snickered at the young man's question. The young man replied, "In fact, cold does *not* exist. According to the laws of physics, what we consider cold is in reality the absence of heat. Every body or object is susceptible to study when it has or transmits energy, and heat is what makes a body or matter have or transmit energy. Absolute zero (-460 F), is the total absence of heat, and all matter becomes inert and incapable of reaction at that temperature. Cold does not exist. We have created this word to describe how we feel if we have no heat."

The student continued, "Professor, does darkness exist?"

The professor responded, "Of course it does."

The student replied, "Once again, you are wrong, sir. Darkness does not exist, either. Darkness is, in reality, the absence of light. Light we can study—but not darkness. In fact, we can use Newton's prism to break white light into many colors and study the various wavelengths of each color. You cannot measure darkness. A simple ray of light can break into a world of darkness and illuminate it. How can you know how dark a certain space is? You measure the amount of light present. Isn't that correct? Darkness is the term used by man to describe what happens when there is no light present."

Finally, the young man asked the professor, "Sir, does evil exist?"

Now uncertain, the professor responded, "Of course, as I have already said. We see it everyday. It is in the daily examples of man's inhumanity to man. It is in the multitude of crime and violence everywhere in the world. These manifestations are nothing else but evil."

To this, the student replied, "Evil does not exist, sir, or at least it does not exist unto itself. Evil is simply the absence of God. It is just like darkness and cold, a word that man has created to describe the absence of God. God did not create evil. Evil is the result of what happens when man does not have God's love present in his heart. It's like the cold that comes when there is no heat or the darkness that comes when there is no light."

The professor sat down.

In Opposition to God, Satan Hates Mankind

Even before the creation, God existed. Subordinate to God were three archangels: Lucifer, Michael, and Gabriel. For eons, Lucifer was the favored prince of all angelic beings. He was gifted, ardent, and devoted. He was brilliant, imperial, and passionate. He was the most adored in heaven. His position was second only to God himself…until the moment he learned of God's new creation. God's new creation was of a new race that was not angelic. He was creating man in His image for fellowship, worship, and praise. On learning of God's new creation, pride swelled up inside Lucifer. The Bible says that "iniquity was found in him." As God is a holy God, he could not look upon Lucifer's iniquity. So as the story goes, Lucifer was thrown away from heaven and given a new name—Satan—and he was cursed.

Satan's pride, jealousy, and anger turned to hatred of this new creation that usurped God's attention. He was determined to come between God and mankind. God's heart was and is to fellowship with and to receive praise from mankind. As God receives praise and honor, His heart was and is to bless mankind.

Satan's heart was and is filled with hatred for mankind. He wants to interfere with the fellowship between God and mankind. His desire is to kill, steal, and destroy.

Key to health—Recognize the author of sickness and disease.

"A thief does not come, except to steal and kill and destroy; I have come that they might have life, and have it abundantly" (John 10:10, Lamsa).

"Concerning Jesus of Nazareth, whom God anointed with the Holy Spirit and with power, and who, because God was with Him, went about doing good and healing all who were oppressed by the devil" (Acts 10:38, Lamsa).

Satan's deception left us with a choice. The consequences of our choice are seen in...

The Fruits of the Trees in the Garden

Most are familiar with the Biblical story of Adam and Eve in the Garden of Eden. Central in the garden stood the Tree of the Knowledge of Good and Evil. This tree produced the "forbidden fruit." The account is that Satan, in the form of a snake, tempted Adam and Eve to eat by implying that they would then have the knowledge to be gods themselves. Perhaps this planted a seed of doubt about God's motives in telling them not to eat of this tree "or they would surely die." Their thoughts became self-centered instead of God-centered, and they ate.

After eating, they began to have revelations. They were naked! They were embarrassed. They were ashamed. They were then fearful of the loving God that sought them in the garden. They felt guilt. They started blaming each other *and* the snake.

Those emotions were not part of life before they disobeyed God and ate the forbidden fruit. Their disobedience started a slow death characterized by emotional instability, fear, and separation from God.

According to scripture, the fruits of a self-centered life (the Tree of the Knowledge of Good and Evil) include rejection, hatred, violence, jealousy, envy, condemnation, shame, pride, guilt, lying, lust, greed, covetousness, revenge, retaliation, slander, critical spirit, fear, terror, un-forgiveness, unmerciful, self-pity, gossip, and the like.

Imagine if God had left Adam and Eve in the Garden of Eden and permitted them to eat of the Tree of Life… after having the fruit of the Tree of the Knowledge of Good and Evil. They would have lived an eternal double-minded existence. Satan would have won. Man would have been eternally outcast by God because he cannot fellowship with iniquity. God is too holy. Our fellowship would have been eternally destroyed.

As Christians, we have the opportunity in Christ Jesus to be forgiven and to eat the fruits of the Tree of Life. Jesus, God's only begotten son, the perfect sacrifice, was beaten, crucified, and died for you. He then rose from the dead. He conquered sin and death for you so that you could, by accepting Him, live with him eternally. It was by the stripes of his beating that he obtained our healing. It is by accepting Him, dying to ourselves, and letting Him take charge of our lives that we have eternal life. When we let Christ be Lord and direct our lives we are eating from the Tree of Life.

God can now look upon us through the blood of Jesus. We can eat of the Tree of Life. We can bear the fruits of the God-centered life and fellowship with God eternally. All praise, honor, and glory to Jesus our Savior!

When we choose to live the God-centered life, the fruits are very different from those previously listed. The God-centered life leads to love, joy, peace, long-suffering, goodness, gentleness, faith, virtue, purity, wisdom, justice, honesty, fairness, sincerity, knowledge, understanding, grace, mercy, excellence, forgiveness, compassion, devotion, and truth.

The decisions we make every day of our lives will lead to very specific results. Jesus summed it up in Mark 12:30-31(NIV): "Love the Lord your God with all your heart and with all your soul and with all your mind and with all your strength. The second one is this: 'Love your neighbor as yourself.' There is no commandment greater than these."

1. Putting anything, including ourselves, ahead of those commands has consequences spiritually, emotionally, and physically.

2. God created us with free will. We choose each day whom we will serve. We become a servant of whom we choose to serve—God or Satan. The evidence of whom we choose to serve is manifest in the fruits of our lives. It is our choice.

Action step—In some of the actions steps I suggest further readings that delve deeper into specific topics. I would encourage you to first finish *Revelations in a Brown Paper Bag* to get a general understanding before deviating to these more in-depth studies. Consider reading *Biblical Foundations of Freedom: Destroying Satan's Lies With God's Truth* by Art Mathias. Also read *There Were Two Trees in the Garden* by Rick Joyner. Both of these books are empowering and faith building!

Key to health—Knowing your body is the Temple of the Holy Spirit

Revelations in a Brown Paper Bag

Or do you not know that your body is the temple of the Holy Spirit that dwells within you, which you have of God, and you are not your own? For you have been bought with a price; therefore glorify God in your body and your spirit, because they belong to God.

> 1 Corinthians 6:19, 20 (Lamsa)

"Liberty not only means that the individual has both the opportunity and the burden of choice; it also means that he must bear the consequences of his actions...Liberty and responsibility are inseparable."

> —F.A. Hayek (1899-1992) [3]

Dr. Gary H. Coller

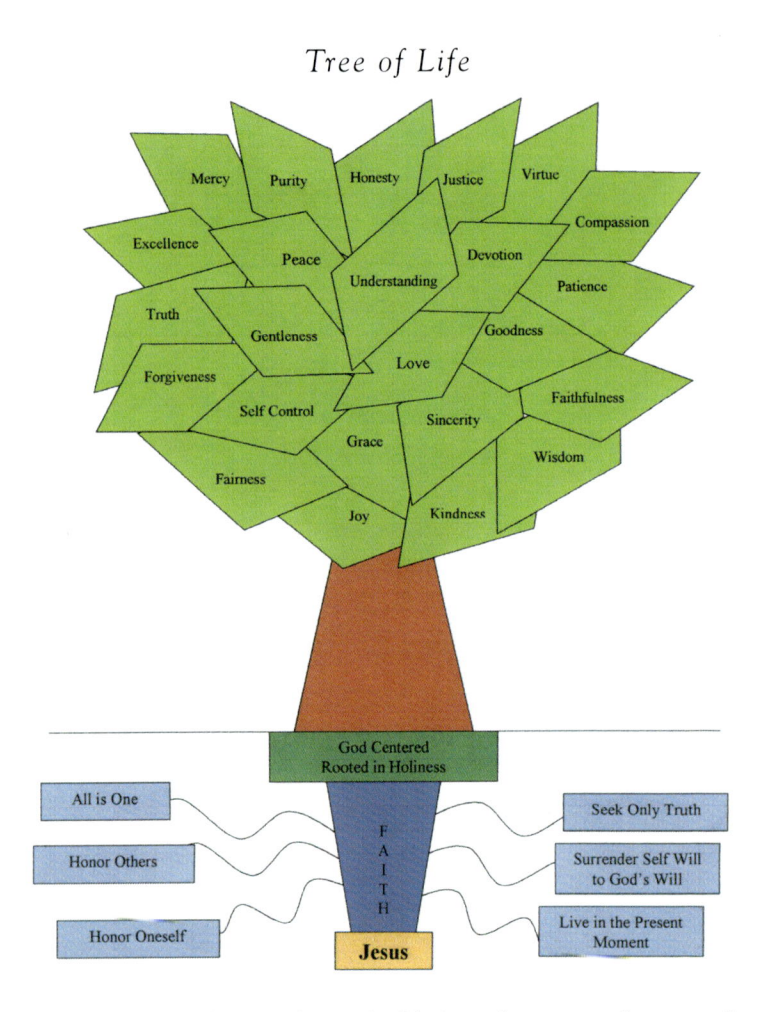

Tree of Life

Leaves: Mercy, Purity, Honesty, Justice, Virtue, Excellence, Compassion, Peace, Devotion, Understanding, Patience, Truth, Gentleness, Goodness, Forgiveness, Love, Self Control, Faithfulness, Sincerity, Grace, Fairness, Wisdom, Joy, Kindness

Trunk top: God Centered Rooted in Holiness

Trunk: F A I T H — Jesus

Branches: All is One, Honor Others, Honor Oneself, Seek Only Truth, Surrender Self Will to God's Will, Live in the Present Moment

"I can do all things through Christ who strengthens me" (Philippians 4:13. Lamsa).

The Tree of Life is founded in Jesus. Its roots are holy truths. As we become holy, God communes with us more intimately, and He manifests His fruits in our lives.

We can choose to live life abundantly, reigning with God and enjoying the fruits of the Tree of Life, or we can choose to reach down into the muck of Satan's diseased world. We can choose to suffer the consequences and bear the fruits of the Tree of the Knowledge of Good and Evil.

The Tree of the Knowledge of Good and Evil is founded in self-centered existence and is characterized by pride, fear, greed, lust, gluttony, anger, envy, and laziness. The roots of a self-centered life block our connection to God's vital energy. His spirit is not manifest in our lives. The fruits are much different.

Key to health—Godly wisdom

> Who is wise among you and has training? Let him prove his words by his good deeds in the humbleness of wisdom. But if you have bitter envying among you or strife in your heart, do not boast and do not lie against the truth. This wisdom does not come from above, but it is earthly, sensual, devilish. For wherever envy and strife are, there is confusion

and every sort of evil. But the wisdom that is from above is first pure, then full of peace, and is gentle, obedient, full of mercy and good fruits, without partiality, and without hypocrisy. And the fruit of righteousness is sown in peace by the peacemakers.

James 3:13-18 (Lamsa)

Key to health—Being rooted in Christ

"And they have no root in themselves, but last for a while; and when trouble or persecution comes because of the Word they soon stumble" (Mark 4:17, Lamsa).

Key to health—No fear

Fear empowers the works of the enemy, just like faith empowers the works of Jesus.

"For the thing which I greatly feared has come upon me, and that which I was afraid of has befallen me" (Job 3:25, Lamsa).

Revelations in a Brown Paper Bag

Tree of the Knowledge of Good and Evil

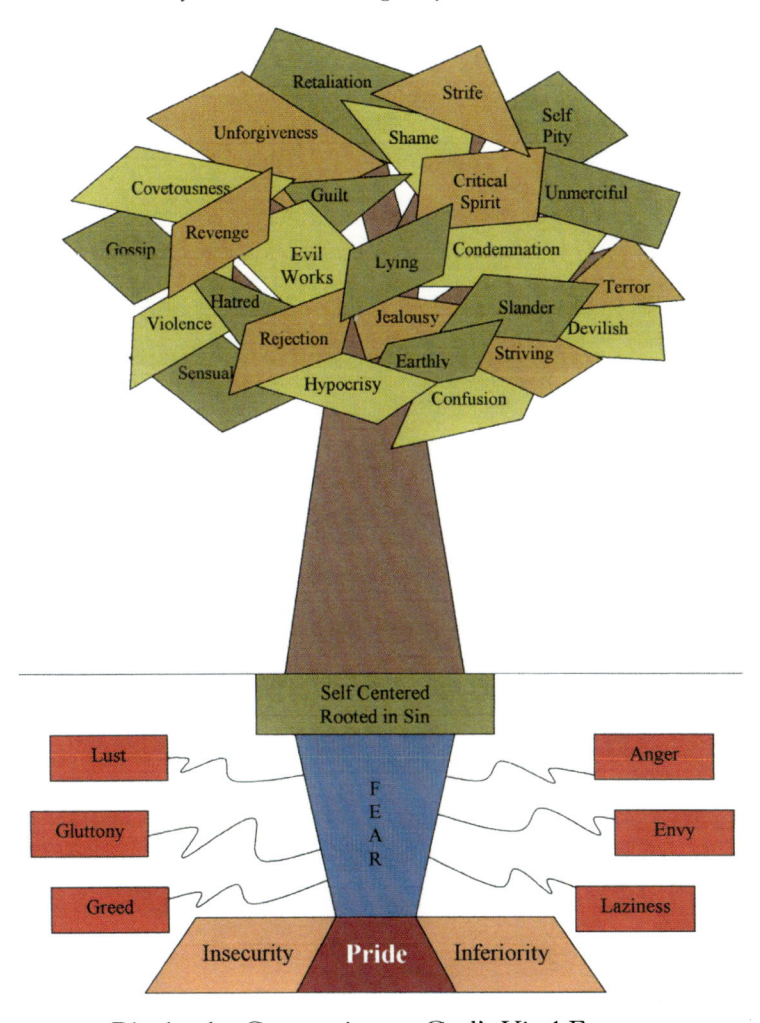

Retaliation, Strife, Self Pity, Unforgiveness, Shame, Covetousness, Guilt, Critical Spirit, Unmerciful, Gossip, Revenge, Evil Works, Lying, Condemnation, Terror, Hatred, Jealousy, Slander, Devilish, Violence, Rejection, Striving, Sensual, Earthly, Hypocrisy, Confusion

Self Centered Rooted in Sin

Lust, Gluttony, Greed

FEAR

Anger, Envy, Laziness

Insecurity — **Pride** — Inferiority

Blocks the Connection to God's Vital Energy

47

Pride directs our focus from God to ourselves. When we focus on ourselves we compare ourselves to our perceptions of others and often to our own perceived failures and shortcomings. The roots of inferiority and insecurity grow. We become fearful. Fear blocks our connection to Gods vital energy and the fruits of our life are those demonstrated in the Tree of the Knowledge of Good and Evil. In other words, when we focus on ourselves and how we measure up to an ideal we always fall short. We start to die. When we focus on God's grace (unmerited favor) and his forgiveness we reconnect to his energy and we are restored.

Pastor Henry Wright, in his book *A More Excellent Way*, discusses the spiritual roots of disease.[4] Sometimes, the way to healing is not a prescription, surgery, or even better nutrition and/or exercise. These are often necessary to "manage a disease." Instead, healing results when we change our decisions, attitudes, and emotions. By doing so, we can hope to prevent and eradicate disease!

Perhaps the most important negative emotion we encounter is trouble forgiving ourselves and others. We feel justified in our anger. Please understand, when you harbor un-forgiveness, it hurts you. It can turn into bitterness, which scripture says is like achiness to our bones. Could this be a root of arthritis? Un-forgiveness can lead to anxiety. Could this be a root of ulcers, etc.?

In his book *A More Excellent Way*, Pastor Wright gives many examples of negative emotions leading to specific health problems. When people deal with the negative emotions, the testimonies verify that healings follow.

As the Bible says in Matthew 6:33 (Lamsa), "Seek first the Kingdom of God and His righteousness, and all these things will be added unto you." If we choose to obey God and to make decisions that honor Him, we receive His blessings. If, on the other hand, we reject God's ways and travel our own self-centered path, the resulting unforgiveness, bitterness, fear, and other negative emotions will destroy us.

Action step—If you want to be healed and remain healthy, forgive yourself and others. Do not harbor negative emotions. Ask God for his help. He is faithful. You might also make a list of those you have offended. Seek God on how to restore fellowship. Pray. Ask God for guidance. Make another list of those that have offended you. Ask God for His help to give you the strength to forgive them. Pray for them. I have found it hard to stay angry with someone when I take time to pray for them. Pastor Henry Wright's book, *A More Excellent Way*, is a wonderful resource to assist you in this endeavor.

> "People are often unreasonable, illogical, and self-centered, forgive them anyway. If you are kind, people may accuse you of selfish, ulterior motives; be kind anyway. If you are successful, you will win some false friends and some true enemies; succeed anyway. If you are honest and frank, people may cheat you; be honest and frank anyway. What you spend years building, someone may destroy overnight; build anyway. If you find sincerity and happiness, they may be jealous; be happy anyway. The good you do today, people will often forget tomorrow; do good anyway. Give the world the best you have, and it may never be enough; give the world the best you have anyway. You see, in the final analysis, it is all between you and God; it was never between you and them, anyway."
>
> —Mother Theresa of Calcutta,
> "The Final Analysis" [5]

The God-Centered Life

The God-centered life is a choice. We are justified by faith, but then the sanctification process begins. When you fail, return to God and repent. That means do an "about face" Turn back from your error. God is faithful to forgive you. He is grateful that you learned another lesson. "No one is good. Not one," according to scripture. As we let Jesus be center of our lives, we become better each day. We become more like Him. That is what sanctification is all about (letting Jesus shine through us) that we become more like Him. What a blessing we have in Jesus!

Key to health—Fear and worship God

"Be not wise in your own eyes; revere the Lord, and depart from evil. It shall be healing to your flesh and marrow to your bones" (Proverbs 3:7-8, Lamsa).

"Reverence for the Lord prolongs life; but the years of the wicked shall be shortened" (Proverbs 10:27, Lamsa).

God inhabits His praises, so praise God to get close to God. God's Word is His will, so dwell in the word to know His will for you.

The spoken word has power, and faith comes by hearing the Word. If you desire to go to another level in Christ, I highly recommend getting a recorded version of the Bible and play it in your home night and day—whenever possible, hear His Word. Let His truth bathe you even as you sleep. As you do this, He will draw closer to you, and you will begin to experience Him. He will manifest in your life.

Because I can't do this for you, the next best faith builder is a compilation of scripture for you to read. But remember, to understand scripture, we must first have faith in God. This results in God illuminating His Word to us. The scripture will then take on life. In faith, dwell on these verses. Take the time to read them slowly. God promises that His Word will not return void.

> And whatsoever you do in word or deed, do all in the name of the Lord Jesus, giving thanks to God and the Father by him.
>
> Colossians 3:16-17 (KJV)

> I love them that love me; and those that seek me early shall find me.
>
> Proverbs 8:17 (KJV)

> Seek the Lord and His strength, seek his face continually. Remember his marvelous works that he

hath done, his wonders, and the judgment of his mouth.

> 1 Chronicles 16:11-12 (KJV)

You are my friends, if you do whatsoever I command you. Henceforth, I call you not servants; for the servant knows not what his Lord does: but I have called you friends; for all things that I have heard of my Father I have made known unto you. You have not chosen me, but I have chosen you, and ordained you, that you should go and bring forth fruit, and that your fruit should remain: that whatsoever you shall ask of the Father in My name, He shall give it to you.

> John 15:14-16 (KJV)

Speaking to yourselves in psalms and hymns and spiritual songs, singing and making melody in your heart to the Lord; Giving thanks always for all things unto God and the Father in the name of our Lord Jesus Christ.

> Ephesians 5:19-20 (KJV)

I will bless the Lord at all times: His praise shall continually be in my mouth. My soul shall make her boast in the Lord: the humble shall hear thereof, and be glad. O magnify the Lord with me, and let us exalt His name together. I sought the Lord, and He heard me, and He delivered me from all my fears.

Psalms 34:1-4 (KJV)

O God thou art my god; early will I seek you: my soul thirsts for you, my flesh longs for you in a dry and thirsty land, where no water is. To see the power and the glory, so I have seen you in the sanctuary. My soul shall be satisfied as with marrow and fatness; and my mouth shall praise you with joyful lips: when I remember you on my bed and meditate on you in the night watches. Because you have been my help, therefore in the shadow of your wing I will rejoice.

Psalm 63:1-2, 5-7 (KJV)

But put you on the Lord Jesus Christ, and make not provision for the flesh, to fulfill the lusts thereof

Romans 13:14 (KJV)

So will I sing praise unto thy name forever, that I may daily perform my vows.

Psalm 61:8 (KJV)

In thee, O Lord, do I put my trust: let me never be put to confusion. For thou are my hope, O Lord God: thou are my trust from my youth. Let my mouth be filled with your praise and your honor all the day.

Psalm 71:1, 5, 8 (KJV)

Trust in Him at all times; you people, pour out your heart before Him: God is a refuge for us. Selah.

Psalm 62:8 (KJV)

Let them shout for joy, and be glad, that favour my righteous cause: yea, let them say continually, let the Lord be magnified, which has pleasure in the prosperity of His servant. And my tongue shall speak of the righteousness and thy praise all the day long.

Psalm 35:27-28 (KJV)

It is a good thing to give thanks unto the Lord, and to sing praises unto His name, O most high: To shew forth thy loving kindness in the morning and thy faithfulness every night, through thy work: I will triumph in the works of thy hands.

Psalm 9:1, 2, 4 (KJV)

Sing unto the Lord, bless His name; shew forth his salvation from day to day.

Psalm 96:2 (KJV)

From the rising of the sun unto the going down of the same the Lord's name is to be praised.

Psalm 113:3 (KJV)

I will delight myself in thy statutes: I will not forget thy word. Make me to understand the way of thy precepts: so shall I talk of thy wondrous works.

Psalm 119:16, 27 (KJV)

My soul waits for the Lord more than they that watch for the morning: I say more than they that watch for the morning. Let Israel hope in the Lord: for with the Lord there is mercy, and with him is plenteous redemption.

Psalm 130:6-7 (KJV)

I will sing unto the Lord as long as I live: I will sing praise to my God while I have my being. My meditation of Him shall be sweet: I will be glad in the Lord.

Psalm 103:33-34 (KJV)

By Him therefore let us offer the sacrifice of praise to God continually, that is, the fruit of our lips giving thanks to his name.

Hebrews 13:15 (KJV)

Thou will keep Him in perfect peace, whose name is stayed on thee: because he trusts in thee.

Isaiah 26:3 (KJV)

And He said to them all, "If any man will come after Me, let him deny himself, and take up His cross daily, and follow Me. For whosoever will save his life shall lose it: but whosoever will lose his life for my sake, the same shall save it. For what profit is it to a man, if he gains the whole world, and is himself destroyed or lost?"

Luke 9a:23-25 (KJV)

Be merciful unto me, O Lord: for I cry unto thee daily. Rejoice the soul of the servant: for unto thee, O Lord, do I lift up my soul. For thou, Lord, art good, and ready to forgive; and plenteous in mercy unto all them that call upon thee.

Psalm 86:3-5 (KJV)

Keep me safe, O God, for in you I take refuge. I said to my Lord, 'You are my Lord; apart from you I have no good thing.' As for the saints who are in the land, they are the glorious ones in whom is all my delight. The sorrows of those will increase who run after other Gods. I will not pour out their libations of blood or take up their names on my lips. Lord, you have assigned me my portion and my cup; you have made my lot secure. The boundary lines have fallen for me in pleasant places; surely I have a delightful inheritance. I will praise the Lord, who counsels me; even at night my heart instructs me. I have set the Lord always before me. Because He is at my right hand, I will not be shaken. Therefore my heart is glad and my tongue rejoices; my body will also rest secure, because you will not abandon me to the grave, nor will you let your holy one see decay. You have made known to me the path of life; you will fill me with joy in your presence, with eternal pleasures at your right hand.

Psalms 16:1-11 (KJV)

"For in Him we live, and move, and have our being" (Acts 17:28, KJV)…the God-centered life!

Try to make a small adjustment in your view of your relationship with God. We often consider ourselves as sinners saved by grace. We are forever striving to obtain a relationship with God. We are trying to live up to the law. This type of sanctification can never be fully obtained. Paul said in Galatians 2:16 (KJV),

> "Knowing that man is not justified by the works of the law, but by faith in Jesus Christ, even we have believed in Christ Jesus, that we might be justified by faith in law; for by the works of the law no flesh shall be justified."

That is why Jesus came—not to abolish the law—He came to fulfill it. Now that you have asked Jesus into your heart to be your Lord and Savior, that spark of faith will energize your spirit…like light shining in the darkness. It is the spark of faith in Christ that ignites the core spiritual being to manifest the Holy Spirit within us. Your faith will grow as you nurture it with the word. God's light will shine through you. This will happen despite your striving. Just keep your eyes on Jesus, build your faith with the Word, and you will be transformed. It is all about Jesus! Now that you are saved, Jesus is your savior. Now make Him Lord of your life (master, ruler, boss, absolute control—He is in charge!) and you reign with Him in His kingdom. You have the choice (free will) to reach back down out of glory into the muck of sin. You can get dirty. It is your choice. It is also your choice to repent and turn from your sin. Get washed in His blood. Then, like the father of the prodigal son, God will take you back and bless you.

> …May grace (God's unmerited favor) be granted to you and spiritual peace (the place of Christ's kingdom) from Him who is and who was and who is to come, and from the seven spirits-that is the seven fold holy spirit-before His throne, and from Jesus Christ the faithful and trustworthy witness, the first born of the dead (that is, the first to be brought back to life) and the Prince (ruler) of the kings of the earth. To Him who ever loves us and has once (for all) loosed and freed us from our sins by His own blood, and formed us into a kingdom (a royal race), priests to His God and Father, to Him be the glory and the power and the majesty and the dominion throughout the ages and forever and ever. Amen.
>
> Revelations 1:4-6 (AMP)

In the book *Walking in the Covenant of Salt* by Ron Miller, he uses the analogy of bread as being the grace we receive by faith in Jesus Christ. He refers to the salt as being our personal righteousness. A doctrine of bread without salt may result in salvation, but the Bible says in James 2:18 (NLT) "How can you show me your faith if you don't have good deeds? I will show you my faith by my good deeds." A doctrine of salt without bread is also dead because it implies that we must work our way to heaven. "No one is good. Not one." When personal righteousness is exacted as the means of attaining God, death will rule. You cannot work your way into heaven. The attempt to do so is referred to as Pharisees' spirit, a religious spirit that Jesus condemned. True holiness, power, and revival are found when the bread is salted.

This concept is further demonstrated by understanding the difference between the old and new covenants. An analogy of the old covenant (the law) concept could be found if I told you, "Don't think of a pink elephant." What is your first thought?…A pink elephant, right? Under the law we are told what we can't do. We must work to resist. In the new covenant (grace) God works from within us. Without being told, we don't normally think about pink elephants.

Faith in God permits Him to work from the inside. As He changes us, we proceed toward righteousness. Our desire will be to please God and live a holy life.

An analogy to explain the "salt covenant" is found in laser energy. Normal light is made up of many wavelengths traveling each in their own direction. The laser coordinates the light rays to a specific focused wavelength, creating incredible energy. As God works through us to clean out the competing self-centered wavelengths, His pure, focused light can shine through. We then experience the power of God's perfect will.

Action step—I encourage you to read *Walking in the Covenant of Salt* by Ron Miller. This book develops a balanced understanding of the covenants God has made with His covenant people.

Key to health—Serve the Lord

> And you shall serve the Lord your God, and He shall bless your bread and your water; and I will take sickness away from your houses. There shall nothing cast their young nor be barren in your land; the number of your days I will fulfill.
>
> Exodus 23:25-26 (Lamsa)

But now Jesus Christ has received a ministry which is greater than that; just as the covenant in which He was made a mediator is greater, so are the promises greater than those given in the old covenant.

Hebrews 8:6 (Lamsa)

The Structure of Man

To better understand how health and healing are tied to such kingdom principles, we need to understand the structure of man. The outer shell, our body, is world-consciousness. It is comprised of our senses: seeing, hearing, touching, tasting, and smelling. It may yield to indulgence and sensuality, which is part of what we have referred to as a self-centered life. The body is subject to physical systems, strength, and disorder. It may become broken, diseased, and afflicted. It may become self serving or God pleasing.

The soul has different characteristics. It is our self-consciousness. It is comprised of our intellect: the mind, thought and reason. It may yield to unbelief, confusion, etc. It is here that emotions are found. Emotions include: feelings, temperament, and concerns. It is our source of will—choices and actions. It may yield to disobedience.

Centered in man's structure is our spirit. It is our God-consciousness comprised of faith, hope, and love. Faith is our assurance, and it is our stability. It is fed by the Word of God. Hope is our confidence—our expectancy. Hope is sustained by looking to Jesus. Love is our communication. It is our motivation. Love is nurtured by the flow of the Holy Spirit. The gifts of the Holy Spirit include: the word of wisdom, the word of knowledge, the gift of faith, the gift of healing, the working of miracles, the gift of prophecy, discernment between true and false spirits, the gift of speaking in tongues, and the gift of interpretation of tongues.

Key to health—Love

> Though I speak with the tongues of men and of angels, but have not love, I have become sounding brass or a clanging cymbal. And though I have the gift of prophecy, and understand all mysteries and all knowledge, and though I have all faith, so that I could remove mountains, but have not love, I am nothing. And though I bestow all my goods to feed the poor, and though I give my body to be burned, but have not love it profits me nothing.

Love suffers long and is kind; love does not envy; love does not parade itself, it is not puffed up; does not behave rudely, does not seek its own, is not provoked, thinks no evil; does not rejoice in iniquity, but rejoices in the truth; bears all things, believes all things, endures all things. Love never fails. But whether there are prophecies, they will fail; whether there are tongues, they will cease; whether there is knowledge, it will vanish away. For we know in part and we prophesy in part, but when that which is perfect has come, then that which is in part will be done away. When I was a child, I spoke as a child, I thought as a child; but when I became a man, I put away childish things. For now we see in a mirror, dimly but then face to face. Now I know in part, but then I shall know just as I also am known. And now abide faith, hope, love, these three; but the greatest of these is love.

1 Corinthians 13: 1-13 (NKJV)

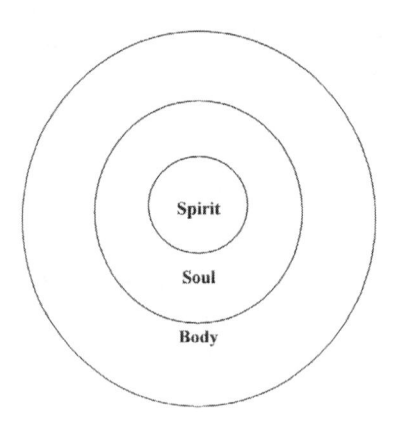

Diagram: three concentric circles labeled Spirit (innermost), Soul (middle), Body (outer).

As you can see in the diagram, man is made up of the spirit, soul, and body. They are independent, yet very dependent on each other. Health and healing encompass all three. Jesus said, and it is clear from the diagram, "The kingdom of God is within you" (Luke 17:21, KJV). God is love, and there is great power as we learn to let that love permeate and shine through us to others. Love covers a multitude of sins. Love heals all wounds. Love brings meaning and life to the other spiritual gifts.

Action step—Read *The Agape Road* by Bob Mumford to better understand walking within God's love.

Love Meter

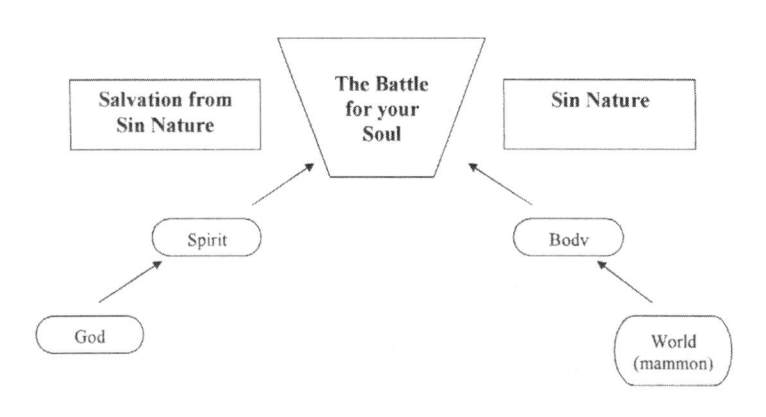

```
[Salvation from Sin Nature] → Spirit → [The Battle for your Soul] ← Body ← [Sin Nature]
                              ↑                                        ↑
                            God                                   World (mammon)
```

"You cannot serve God and mammon" (Matthew 6:24, KJV). A double-minded man is unstable in all he does" (James 1:8, KJV).

Key to health—Do not be double-minded

> If any of you lack wisdom, let him ask of God, who gives to all men liberally and with grace, and it will be given him. But let him ask in faith, not doubting. For he who doubts is like the waves of the sea driven by the wind and tossed. Thus let not that man suppose that he will receive anything of the

Lord. A double-minded man is unstable in all his ways.

James 1:5-8 (Lamsa)

WHOM DO YOU LOVE?

Hot...................**Luke Warm**..................**Cold**
(Love God above all else) (Double-Minded) (Love all else)

God is love (Agape, Pure).
Yet everything done in love (general term)
is not necessarily God…
We must investigate our motives and fruits.

Soul Power

"…the Joy of the Lord is your strength…" Nehemiah 8:10 (KJV)

Life Energy

I have referred to the Tree of Life as the God-centered life that brings in the fruits of health and healing. The roots of the Tree of Life contain energy.

- The energy of God that flows into physical manifestations

- The energy of God as we understand the intelligence of God

- The energy of wisdom and the contact point between God's mind and human thought

- The energy of the power of judgment

- The energy of the love and mercy of God

- The energy of compassion, harmony, and beauty

- The energy of the majesty of God

- The energy of the endurance of God

- The energy of the procreative force of God

- The energy of the community of God—mankind

Energy is power. At the first level, we learn how to handle group identity found in the family or community at large. At later levels, we learn to individualize and manage our spirit, soul, and body. Every choice we make motivated by faith or fear will direct our spirit. If a person's spirit is directed by fear, then fear is manifested in the energy fields of the soul and body. If the person's spirit is directed by faith, then grace returns positive energy to nourish the soul and body. Releasing one's spirit into the physical world through fear or negativity is a truly faithless act of choosing a self-centered life over a God-centered life.

We are spirit, soul, and body. Each is intricately tied to the other. When we hold on to such false Gods as fear, anger, and attachments to the past, it will drain energy from us—spirit, soul, and body! What drains one, drains all. What fuels one, fuels all. The fuel is not found so much in our DNA as it is found in the energy we permit to flow into us through the roots of the Tree of Life!

Please understand that misdirecting the power of your spirit will generate consequences manifested in your soul and body. Know that we all will experience challenges that test our allegiance to God. These tests may come in a variety of forms—loss of wealth, family, friends, health, or worldly power. Such loss activates a potential faith crisis. You must decide who or what you have faith in. Like Jesus on the cross after being forsaken, the Lord Jesus responded, "Into your hands I commend my spirit" (Luke 23:46, KJV). In your crisis, into who's hands do you commend your spirit?

It is in choosing God that we direct our spirit toward health and healing. We must release the past, cleanse the spirit in the blood of Jesus, and return to the present more energized to health and healing.

We have both external energy sources and internal energy sources. The external energy is represented by the Christian sacraments of baptism, communion, and confirmation. The internal energy is represented by marriage, confession, ordination, and the sacrament of extreme unction. Each sacrament relates to a specific sacred truth.

External Energy Sources	Sacred Truth
Baptism	All is one
Communion	Honor one another
Confirmation	Honor oneself

Internal energy sources	Sacred Truth
Marriage	Love is God power
Confession	Surrender self will to Gods will
Ordination	Seek only the truth
Extreme unction (Anointing of the sick)	Live in the present moment

External Energy Sources
ALL IS ONE

We are interconnected to all of life and to one another. We first experience this in our biological family. We experience the "blood bond." This may expand to a fellowship of believers in the church you attend. We then learn of the connection between ourselves and the rest of humanity. How often have we heard, "What a small world this is," as we are made aware of the close ties we have with others? In violating the energy bonds between ourselves and others, as when we consider those that are different as being less than us, this creates conflict within our spirit, soul, and body.

The sacrament of baptism establishes the commitment to the nurturing of the young person physically and spiritually. Fulfilling that commitment creates a strong foundation of faith and truth, which can be a source of strength throughout life. Baptism also creates a commitment on the part of the young person to accept their family as "God chosen" to teach them life's lessons. They also accept personal responsibility to live honorably in this world, treating others with respect and striving to live the God-centered rather than the self-centered life.

By fulfilling these commitments, we honor our lives. If we renege on the commitments by, for instance, dishonoring our biological family, it depletes a great deal of power from our energy system. Viewing one's family in negative terms depletes power because it opposes the higher truth within the energy system. If we are to attain a higher energy state, we must first honor our families and humanity as a whole.

Key to health—Honor your parents

> Children, obey your parents in the Lord, for this is right. This is the first commandment with promise:

> Honor your father and your mother, that it may be well with you and you may live long on the earth.
>
> Ephesians 6:1-3 (Lamsa)

Key to health—Obey God's commands, not the doctrines of men

> He said to them, the prophet Isaiah well prophesied about you, O hypocrites, as it is written, This people honor me with their lips, but their heart is far away from me. And they worship me in vain when they teach the doctrines of the commandments of men. For you have ignored the commandment of God, and you observe the tradition of men, such as the washing of cups and pots and a great many other things like these. He said to them, You certainly do injustice to the commandment of God so as to sustain your own tradition. For Moses said, Honor your father and your mother; and he who curses father or mother, let him be put to death. But you say, A man may say to his father or his mother, What is left over is Corban (my offering); And yet you do not let him do anything for his father or his mother. So you dishonor the Word of God for the

sake of the tradition which you have established; and you do a great many other things like these.

> Mark 7:6-13 (Lamsa)

HONOR ONE ANOTHER

Communion is an external energy source that gives us the power to act with integrity and honor in our relationships. It resonates into our financial and creative activities. Integrity and honor are necessary for health. Violate our honor, and we contaminate our spirit, soul, and body.

In part, communion signifies that each person we encounter is God's design. When we share communion with someone, we are acknowledging that we are all part of one spiritual family. But each encounter in your life plays an essential role in your development. Your challenge is to become mature enough to see the bigger picture. We will fail to see God's purpose in an encounter if we quickly choose to interpret it negatively, generate negative energy, and view those involved in our painful encounters as our enemies. In the extreme, love the sinner; hate the sin.

Before I receive personal communion I often say this prayer.

> Heavenly Father, I thank you for sending your son, Jesus Christ, to redeem me. I thank you that through Christ's suffering, He purchased a threefold redemption for my spirit, soul, and body. Father, as you have forgiven me, I also forgive those who have sinned against me. Lord, I choose to forgive and release anyone who has wronged me, and I ask you to search my spirit and remove any trace of sin in disobedience from my life. Today, I release from my mental prison anyone who has hurt me in any way, and I ask you to help them spiritually and bless them. Father, as I receive this communion, I ask you to bring strength and health to me spiritually, emotionally, and physically because of the new covenant that was sealed through the sufferings of Christ. Father, Jesus carried my infirmities; therefore, I ask you to lift from me what Jesus has carried for me. I receive it by faith, and I give you all glory and honor in the name of Jesus Christ. Amen.

The bread that we break is the communion of the body of Christ (the new wineskin).

The cup of wine which we bless is the communion of the blood of Christ (the new wine).

I have been crucified with Christ and I no longer live, but Christ lives in me. The life I live in the body, I live by faith in the Son of God, who loved me and gave himself for me. I do not set aside the grace of God, for if righteousness could be gained by the law, Christ died for nothing.

Galatians 2:20-21(AMP)

Key to health—Proper discernment of the Lord's body

Therefore whosoever shall eat of the Lords bread and drink of His cup unworthily shall be guilty of the blood and body of the Lord. For this reason, let a man examine himself and eat of this bread and drink of this cup. For he who eats and drinks unworthily eats and drinks to his condemnation; for he does not discern the Lord's body. This is the reason many are sick and weak among you, and many are dying. For if we would judge ourselves, we would not be judged. But when we are judged by our Lord, we are simply chastened, so that we may not be condemned with the world.

1 Corinthians 11:27-32 (Lamsa)

HONOR ONESELF

As we condemn the self-centered life and exalted the God-centered life, the concept of honoring oneself takes on a vital truth. We must find our identity in Christ. That identity is honorable, yet humble. The meaning behind the sacrament of confirmation is accepting responsibility for the quality of person we become. Confirmation is the process of affirming the inherent goodness of that person. Whether done formally or informally, validation is essential to normal psychological development. When such confirmation is lacking, it manifests as continual need for approval of others, which can lead to unhealthy associations with gangs, cults, and other inappropriate groups.

When we lack self-respect, our relationships become fragile states of intimacy. We fear abandonment. The fear of being alone can determine our actions and can lead to very destructive behaviors.

A lack of confirmation can result in an inability to develop a healthy sense of who we are in Christ. It can interfere with our ability to receive and trust in 'intuitive guidance" from our own spirit. It can block our ability to "hear God"…which is analogous to cutting off the power supply!

We must stay plugged in. Healthy self-esteem found in Christ will give us power and stamina beyond the physical body alone. This power intensifies as we accept our lives.

We lose power when we focus on what is missing in our lives or when we view life as empty or meaningless. This power is intensified as we develop an attitude of gratitude and appreciation for all we have—including life, itself.

"In all things, pray, praise, and give thanks!"

Key to health—Have a happy heart

"A merry heart makes the body healthy; but a broken spirit dries up the bones" (Proverbs 17:22, Lamsa).

Internal Energy Sources
LOVE IS GOD POWER

Love is the energy center of the human energy system. It is represented by the sacrament of marriage. It is the doorway into our internal world. Our entire being (spirit, soul, and body) requires love to survive and thrive.

We violate this energy when we act without love. When we harbor negative emotions for ourselves and others, we poison ourselves at every level. The strongest poison is the inability to forgive ourselves and others. Un-forgiveness disables ones emotional resources.

Key to health—Forgiveness

> And when you stand up to pray, forgive whatever you have against any man, so that your Father in heaven will forgive you your trespasses. But if you will not forgive, even your father in heaven will not forgive you your trespasses.
>
> Mark 11:25-26 (Lamsa)

Action step—Let God's power shine through you to others. Make the effort to forgive. Above all, learn to love unconditionally.

There is power in forgiveness. There is greater power in love! So as God commanded in Mark 12:30-31, love God above all else and love your neighbor as yourself.

We are, by nature, compassionate beings that thrive when we experience tranquility and harmony. These emotions are essential to the development and maintenance of our health. If we are not filled with the vital energies of love, tranquility, and harmony, our hearts are empty.

For this reason, violations of the heart must be rectified. A broken heart need not be terminal. Let Jesus in. Praise God—He loves you!

SURRENDER SELF WILL TO GOD'S WILL

To surrender self-will to God's will is the greatest single act we can perform to bring spiritual stability into our lives. The revelation that God is smarter than us is truly life enhancing. His purposes are greater than ours.

As we grow up, we develop ideas about how we want our life to unfold. We have hopes and dreams. It is the norm to separate from parents, become independent, and start a career. Then something happens that turns our plans upside-down. Whether the problem involves illness, divorce, loss of a job, or some other crisis, we find ourselves questioning our initial plans. We question our ability to fulfill those plans. We feel like a failure and begin to ask questions like, "What am I really meant to do with my life? Why was I born?" If we answer those questions wisely, we will move from the self-centered to the God-centered life. That choice, made with faith, allows God's authority to enter our lives. He reorders our struggles into successes and our wounds into strengths.

The Bible says that, "All things work together for good for those who love God, to those who are the called according to His purpose" (Romans 8:28, NKJV).

As we turn ourselves over to God for Him to take charge and direct our lives, some housekeeping will be inevitable. He must fill us with His truths and purge us of untruths.

The sacrament of confession deals with the knowledge that it is against our natural makeup to distort truth. The human energy system identifies lies as poison. Our spirit, soul, and body thrive on honesty and integrity. By purging ourselves of lies, we cleanse our spirit so healing can begin. Programs like Alcoholics Anonymous find their very success is the process of confession and turning one's life over to a power greater than themselves. Even psychotherapy is a form of confession. Confession frees the spirit from the bondage of the self-centered existence and redirects it into the God-centered existence.

It is important that our confession does not hurt others. The mandate in Ephesians 4:15 is to speak the truth in love. Confession is intended to direct energy into positive actions and behavior. It is to release ourselves from the burden of negative and guilt-inducing emotions. Confession is not intended to be critical of ourselves or others. We think and speak ill of others out of fear and jealousy, and when we do so, it not only hurts that person but ourselves, as well.

Guess what? Our physical body holds us responsible for this form of destructive behavior. The guilt we experience compels us to seek confession in order to heal. "There are those whose speech is like the piercing of a sword; but the tongue of the wise heals" (Proverbs 12:18, Lamsa).

Key to health—Always speak positive words

> "A man's belly shall be satisfied with the fruits of his mouth; and with the fruits of his lips shall he be filled. Death and life are in the power of the tongue; and those who love it shall eat the fruits thereof" (Proverbs 18:20-21, Lamsa).

> Truly I say to you, whoever should say to the mountain, be moved and fall into the sea, and does not doubt in his heart, but believes that what he says will be done, it will be done to him. Therefore I say to you, anything you pray for and ask, believe that you will receive it, and it will be done for you.
>
> Mark 11:23-24 (Lamsa)

> How long shall this wicked congregation murmur in my presence? I have heard the complaints of the

children of Isreal which they murmur in my presence. Say to them, As I live, says the Lord, as you have spoken in my presence, so will I do to you.

> Numbers 14:27-28 (Lamsa)

Action step—We should *never* intentionally judge another person or ourselves negatively. Negative judgments lead to negative consequences in us, as well as in the external environment!

SEEK ONLY THE TRUTH

Scripture says that "We perish due to a lack of knowledge." What is even more frightening is that "the things we think we know for sure that just are not so." We must be open to new ideas and new revelations as we seek the deeper truths.

Key to health—Knowing and understanding God's Word

> My people are silent for lack of knowledge; because you have rejected knowledge, I will also reject you

from the priesthood; seeing that you have forgotten the law of your God, I will also forget your children.

> Hosea 4:6 (Lamsa)

The sacrament of ordination is officially taking on the role of priest with the life purpose of manifesting what is sacred. In a larger sense, though, we all desire to impact the world in a positive way. We want our lives to be valuable, meaningful, and we want to feel that our lives facilitated the greater good. We want to live in God's blessing to bless others. It is exciting to know that we don't need to be a priest or a pastor to flow in God's energy. We attain ordination when we reach out to family, friends, co-workers, and the like…and we touch their lives in a manner that benefits their personal and/or spiritual growth. Such activities direct God's energy through us to others. When we radiate supportiveness and love we are recognized as possessing God-ordained energy. We become vessels for divine interventions as God's glory shines through us to others!

To truly manifest God's ordained energy, it is necessary to transcend the limitations of human thought—one of the many dichotomies of Biblical revelation. Just like we have to give to get in the material world, it may be necessary to give up some hard-edged absolutes of human reasoning to receive divine understanding. This is what people refer to as "listening with your heart." This is how God's energy transcends human thought, resulting in revelation and mental clarity beyond human reason.

As we turn from the learned tendency to judge, we open ourselves to God-inspired revelation and mental clarity.

LIVE IN THE PRESENT MOMENT

In the God-centered life, it is unnatural to let our thoughts live for too long in the past. Dwelling in the past can interfere with our ability to live in the present; it can interfere with our ability to receive God-inspired revelations each day. God-inspired revelations for today will make little sense if we are focused only on the mysteries of the past. If we live fully in present moment, the past mysteries will be gradually unraveled for us. Remember, unlike our bodies, our spirits are eternal. The more spiritually-centered and focused we become, the more in tune we are with the movement of God. Our bodies are limited by the past, but our God-directed spirit is not. Focus on the present moment. It is at this level that the spiritual energy can supersede the body's energy. In this moment, our bodies can respond to the commands of the spirit. It is in this moment that we thrive, heal, and experience God.

The need to live in the present moment is promoted by the sacrament of extreme unction. The energy associated with this sacrament comes from the ability to release past experiences. If we release the baggage of the past, we have renewed energy for the present. If we choose to live in and dwell on the past, we interfere with the flow of life's energies, and the present becomes distorted by viewing it through the past. This weakens us spirit, soul, and body. We become weakened as we carry the dead from the past into our futures.

Spiritually try to simplify your requirements for healing by making Jesus Christ the center of your life. Try to identify which sacred truth relates to your situation. Organize your internal healing power around learning from the truth. As God leads you, combine God's natural healing energy with functional, alternative, or even conventional medical therapies. Seek the support systems you need. Your task is to move past your wounds—not to live in them. Don't dwell on negatives. Feeling victimized only adds to the problem.

Please remember:

- All situations can be changed in a moment. All illness can be healed. God is not limited by human time, space, or physical concerns.

- Live what you believe. Be consistent. Have faith in God.

- Change is a constant. There is a time for everything under heaven. Every life has phases of difficult and peaceful times. Attempt to go with the flow of change. Don't fight change too aggressively.

- Never look to another for your happiness. Happiness is internal. Happiness is your personal attitude and responsibility.

- Life is a learning experience. Each situation, challenge, and relationship can be a God-given opportunity to learn a lesson to help yourself and others.

- Positive energy is more effective than negative energy every time.

- Live in the present moment. Forgive yourself and others. Learn to let God's love shine through you to others.

Action step—Read *Anatomy of the Spirit: The Seven Stages of Power and Healing* by Caroline Myss, Ph,D. It is a thought-provoking book that condenses consistent thoughts from the world's major religions. The Christian perspective is well documented.

Seven Deadly Sins

Early Christian teachings relate man's tendency to sin. They even refer to the "Seven Deadly Sins"! It is interesting that the "Seven Deadly Sins" correlate closely with the fruits of a self-centered life. The "Seven Deadly Sins" are deadly to our spiritual growth. As the light of our spirit dims, our souls suffer with destructive thoughts and emotions that lead to the decay of our bodies.

Let us examine the "Seven Deadly Sins."

Lust: lust is excessive, even obsessive, thoughts or desires of a sexual nature. Unfulfilled lusts can result in compulsions and/or transgressions such as sexual addiction, adultery, bestiality, and rape. Lust is an excessive desire for sexual release. The other person becomes a "means to an end" for the fulfillment of the subject's lust. The person becomes objectified by the subject's lust.

Gluttony: any form of thoughtless excess can be considered gluttony. Gluttony is an overindulgence of food and/or drink. This sin could include substance abuse and binge drinking, as well.

Greed/Avarice: greed is similar to lust and gluttony in that it is characterized by excess. Greed relates specifically to the acquisition of wealth. Avarice is a more general term for sins, including: disloyalty, betrayal, or treason. It may include violence, trickery, or manipulation inspired by greed. And, as Aquinas once wrote, it is "a sin against God, just as all mortal sins, in as much as man condemns things eternal for the sake of temporal things."

Sloth/Laziness: sloth was defined by Dante as the "failure to love God with all one's heart, all one's mind, and all one's soul." It is characterized by apathy, depression, and joylessness. It is the refusal to enjoy the goodness of God and the world He created. Laziness is the failure to utilize one's talents and gifts. Recall the Biblical story of the servants and the talents. The servant that hid his talents was called wicked. Because of his laziness his talents were taken from him to be given to others. Laziness is characterized as unwillingness to act and unwillingness to care (physically and spiritually).

Wrath/Anger: wrath is defined as uncontrolled and inordinate feelings of anger and hatred. These feelings often lead to vehement denial of truth, self-denial, impatience, desire to seek revenge and generally wishing evil or harm to others. It can also include hatred and intolerance of others for reasons of race or religion, resulting in discrimination. Wrath leads to such things as murder, assault, and genocide. Dante defined wrath as the "love of justice perverted to revenge and spite."[6]

Envy/Jealousy: envy is coveting what someone else has that they perceive that they themselves lack. Dante described this as "love of one's own good perverted to a desire to deprive other men of theirs."[7]

Pride/Hubris/Vanity: pride is considered the original and most serious of the "Seven Deadly Sins." It is the source from which the other sins are derived. It is the sin found in Lucifer that resulted in God turning his back on Lucifer and dispelling him from God's kingdom. Pride is characterized by a desire to be more important or attractive than others and by excessive self-love. This is what we have referred to as the self-centered life.

These "Seven Deadly Sins" have dire consequences. The most important consequence is that these sins take our eyes off of God and place them on ourselves. This results in decay of our spirit, soul, and body.

Key to health—Focus on God, not the cares of this life

"And the thoughts of this world and the deception of wealth and the lusts of other things enter in and choke the word and bear no fruit" (Mark 4:19, Lamsa).

Seven Things the Lord Hates

The "Seven Deadly Sins" take our attention off of God. These are sins that result in God turning His back on us. According to Proverbs 6:16-19, there are seven things that the Lord hates and cannot tolerate. These include: a proud look, a lying tongue, hands that kill innocent people, the mind that thinks up wicked plans, feet that hurry to evil, a lying witness, someone that conjures up trouble between friends.

Key to health—Do not regard iniquity in your heart

"If I regard iniquity in my heart, the Lord will not hear me" (Psalm 66:18, AMP).

It is exciting to know that our tendencies to do the things the Lord hates are curtailed by the love of God shining through into our spirit, enriching our souls, and radiating from our bodies into a hurting world.

As God's spirit shines through us, he replaces lust with chastity, gluttony with abstinence, sloth/laziness with diligence, wrath/anger with patience, envy/jealousy with kindness, and pride/hubris/vanity with humility. Those things He hates will naturally stop, and our fellowship with God will be restored.

It is by faith that the spirit shines through us; it is by faith in Jesus. Accept Him into your heart. Let Him shine through you. Be blessed to be a blessing to others!

Remember, God may permit disease, but it comes from the devil. Exodus 15:26 (KJV) reads, "I will permit to be put upon thee none of the diseases which I have permitted to be brought upon the Egyptians for I am the Lord that healeth thee." Acts 10:38 (KJV) speaks of "how God anointed Jesus of Nazareth with the Holy Ghost and with power, who went about doing good and healing all that were oppressed of the devil." This scripture clearly shows that Jesus is the healer, and Satan is the oppressor.

As we have discussed, God permits us to make the choice to accept or reject His Word. Unbelief focuses on the obstacles. Faith looks to God. God wants all His people to be conquerors. Every Christian should be filled with faith in God's Word and be a conqueror. Every Christian should be bold, wise, and powerful in the Spirit of the Lord. Romans 8:37 (KJV) admonishes us "…in all these things we are more than conquerors through Him who loved us."

Matthew 4:23 tells us that Jesus went teaching, preaching, and healing all kinds of sickness and disease among the people. Let us go and do likewise in the name of "Jesus Christ."

Healing Scriptures

In John 9 (NKJV), Jesus and His disciples passed a blind man. The disciples questioned, "Rabbi, who sinned, this man or his parents, that he was born blind?" Jesus replied, "Neither this man nor his parents sinned, but that the works of God should be revealed in him." The blindness was not due to the sin of the man or his parents. It was the result of the cursed state of man from the Garden of Eden. In his situation, God would reveal His will, His power, and His love by restoring the blind man and setting him free from the curse of blindness. "For this purpose the Son of God has manifested, that He might destroy the works of the devil" (1 John 3:8, NKJV).

God is absolute love. An attribute to that love is that He is always reaching out. He continues to give out of His goodness. God is the same yesterday, today, and tomorrow. Let me emphasize that the "purpose the Son of God has manifested that He might destroy the works of the devil."

Someone once said that prayer is not about overcoming God's reluctance but laying hold of his willingness. This can also be said of healing ministry. It is not about overcoming God's reluctance but laying hold of His willingness to heal. God's willingness can be seen in His Word. In His Word, he has repeatedly revealed his willingness and desire to heal his people. God is the most powerful force in the universe. The Bible says God spoke everything into existence. The Bible also teaches that our words have power. Our confessions impact our lives. When we confess God's own words there is great power. Romans 10:17 (KJV) says, "Faith comes by hearing and hearing by the Word of God." Please read the remainder of this chapter out loud, again and again, and meditate on these healing scriptures until they become a part of your spirit. You can also play the "Healing Scriptures" CD (from Cathedrals of Glory Ministries 616-772-0700). Play it over and over until faith for your healing is established. We have received testimonies from all over the United States of patients being healed after listening repeatedly to the Healing Scriptures! I must emphasize that it is not because I narrated a CD that anyone is healed…it is because God's Word never comes back void that healings occur (Isaiah 55:11). To sample the CD, please visit www.ihcenter.net and click on 'healing scriptures'. Let's get started -

Build Your Faith, Overcome Your Fears

Romans 8:11(NKJV) says, "But if the Spirit of Him who raised Jesus from the dead dwells in you, He who raised Christ from the dead will also give life to your mortal (natural, Earthly) bodies through His Spirit who dwells in you." This is talking about your body that you have now, not the one you're going to receive one day in heaven! Allow the Lord to impart His life into you by placing faith in His Word. Begin to praise Him for this promise. Praise Him for His spirit that dwells in you.

> I have been crucified with Christ-I have shared his crucifixion; it is no longer I who live, but Christ, the Messiah, lives in me; and the life I now live in the body I live by faith-by adherence to and reliance on and trust in the Son of God, who loved me and gave himself up for me.
>
> Galatians 2:20 (AMP)

> Always bearing about in the body the dying of the Lord Jesus (which was for our victory), that the life also of Jesus might be made manifest in our body. For we who live are always delivered unto death for Jesus' sake, that the life also of Jesus might be made manifest in our mortal flesh.
>
> 2 Corinthians 4:10-11(KJV)

Jesus came to set us free from the curse and give us bodily health. Matthew 18:18 (KJV) says, "Verily I say unto you, whatsoever you shall bind on earth shall be bound in heaven: and whatsoever you loose on earth shall be loosed in heaven." The word 'bind' means to forbid, and the word 'loose' means to let go or allow freedom. Do not allow sickness, pain or disease to run free in your body. Bind it or forbid it to stay there any longer. Put your foot down and command it to leave in Jesus's name!

Matthew 6:9-10 (NKJV) says, "Our Father in heaven, hallowed be your name. Your kingdom come, your will be done on earth as it is in heaven." Jesus always prays the will of God, and He prays that the will of God be done here on earth just as it is in heaven. People in heaven are not sick so we can clearly see it is God's will that we also be free from sickness.

Deuteronomy 7:15 (NKJV) says, "And the Lord will take away from you all sickness, and will afflict you with none of the terrible diseases of Egypt which you have known, but will lay them on all those who hate you." If this was a promise to all God's covenant people under the old covenant, how much more does this benefit of health pertain to us today since we are his covenant people in Christ Jesus!

Romans 8:32 (NKJV) says, "He that spared not his own Son, but delivered him up for us all, how shall He not with Him also freely give us all things?" "All things" includes healing!

Mark 16:17 (NKJV) says, "And these signs shall follow them that believe; In my name…they shall lay hands on the sick, and they shall recover." Find someone who believes God's Word regarding healing and have them lay hands on you and pray for you. James 5:16 (KJV) says, "That the effectual fervent prayer of a righteous man avails much."

Isaiah 40:31 (KJV) says, "But they that wait upon the Lord shall renew their strength; they shall mount up with wings as eagles; they shall run and not be weary, and they shall walk and not faint." The word "wait" in this verse implies a positive action of hope based on knowing that the Word of God is a true fact and that it will soon come to pass!

Psalm 34:19 (NKJV) says, "Many are the afflictions of the righteous, but the Lord delivers him out of them all."

Jeremiah 30:17 (KJV) says, "For I will restore health unto thee, and I will heal thee of thy wounds, says the Lord."

Isaiah 53:4-5 (KJV) says,

> Surely He hath borne our griefs (sickness) and carried our sorrows (pains) yet we did esteem Him stricken, smitten of God and afflicted. But He was wounded for our transgressions, He was bruised for our iniquities; the chastisement of our peace was upon Him; and by His stripes we are healed.

This clearly shows that your healing was paid for at the cross!

Jeremiah 33:6 (KJV) says, "Behold, I will bring it health and cure, I will cure them, and will reveal unto them the abundance and truth."

Matthew 18:19 (NKJV) says, "Again I say to you that if two of you agree on earth concerning anything that they ask, it will be done for them by My Father in heaven." The prayer of agreement is powerful. Have someone agree with you for your healing!

Mark 11:24 (NKJV) says, "Therefore I say to you whatever things you ask when you pray, believe that you receive them, and you will have them." "Whatever things" includes healing!

Isaiah 58:8 (NKJV) says, "Thy light shall break forth as the morning, and thy health shall spring forth speedily; and thy righteousness shall go before thee: the glory of the Lord shall be the rear guard."

1 Thessalonians 5:23 (KJV) says, "And the very God of peace sanctify you wholly; and I pray God your whole spirit and soul and body be preserved blameless (sound, complete, and intact) unto the coming of our Lord Jesus Christ." Wholeness, wellness, and health are available for the complete make-up of man- spiritual, soul, and body.

1 Peter 2:24 says, "Who himself bore our sins in His own body on the tree, that we, having died to sins, might live for righteousness—by whose stripes you were healed. Note this is written in past tense. You *were* healed. Jesus did it all. He paid for your total deliverance—spirit, soul, and body!

Psalm 103:2-3 (NKJV) says, "Bless the Lord, O my soul, and forget not all His benefits: Who forgiveth all thine iniquities; who heals all thy diseases." It doesn't say "some," it says "all"! Healing is one of the benefits that belong to the believer along with the benefit of having our sin forgiven.

3 John 2 (NKJV) says, "Beloved, I wish above all things that thou mayest prosper and be in health even as thy soul prospereth."

Jeremiah 17:14 (KJV) says, "Heal me, O Lord, and I shall be healed; save me, and I shall be saved: for thou art my praise." Healing is a finished work, just like salvation, and is paid for at the same time with the same healing blood.

> Is any sick among you? Let him call for the elders of the church; and let them pray over him, anointing him with oil in the name of the Lord: and the prayer of faith will save the sick, and the Lord shall raise him up; and if he has committed sins, they shall be forgiven him.
>
> James 5:14-15(KJV)

You Have Authority in Christ—Resist Fear!

John 10:10 (KJV) says, "The thief [Satan] does not come except to steal, and to kill, and to destroy. I [Jesus] have come that they may have life, and that they may have it more abundantly."

Here we see the will of the Lord for every believer is that we experience abundant life. Jesus came for this very purpose. We also see clearly here that it is not God who afflicts us. Satan afflicts us. The word here for life is the Greek word "Zoe." One commentator describes the true meaning of this word in this verse as "the highest and best of which Christ is."[8] Sickness and disease are not part of the abundant life in Christ. Sickness and disease are truly not "the highest and best of which Christ is."

Luke 10:19 (KJV) says, "Behold, I give unto you power [authority] to tread on serpents and scorpions, and over all the power of the enemy: and nothing shall by any means hurt you." This is an exciting verse. Jesus said He has given us authoritative power over *all*—not just *some* of the enemy! Command Satan to take his hands off of you. Command sickness and disease to leave you now in Jesus's name.

Isaiah 41:10 says, "So do not fear, for I am with you; do not be dismayed, for I am your God. I will strengthen you and help you; I will uphold you with my righteous right hand."

"No weapon formed against you shall prosper, and every tongue which rises against you in judgment you shall condemn. This is the heritage (birthright) of the servants of the Lord, and their righteousness is from Me," says the Lord in Isaiah 54:17 (NKJV). Sickness is judging you falsely. It is part of the curse Jesus was crucified to overcome. It is your birthright to live in health. You condemn it with the Word of God and command it to leave your body.

You Are An Overcomer!

1 John 4:4 (KJV) says, "…greater is he that is in you, than he that is in the world."

1 John 5:4 (KJV) states, "For whatsoever is born of God overcometh the world: and this is the victory that overcometh the world, even our faith." As a believer, we, through Christ, are given the right to overcome that which comes against us. We do not deny that the problem or circumstance exists. We do, however, deny the problem the right to stay! Faith in God is victory all of the time!

Romans 8:31 (KJV) says, "What shall we then say to these things? If God be for us, who can be against us?" You are victorious through Christ. Begin to see yourself the way God sees you.

> As His divine power has given to us all things that pertain to life and godliness, through the knowledge of Him who called us by glory and virtue, by which have been given to us exceedingly great and precious promises, that through these you may be partakers of the divine nature, having escaped the corruption that is in the world through lust.
>
> 2 Peter 1:3-4 (NKJV)

The blessing of health was purchased for us at the cross. The Word of God says it belongs to you now. Your healing must be rooted on the Word of God, not on what you see or how you feel.

Romans 5:17 (kjv) says, "For if by the one man's offense [Adam] death reigned through the one, much more those who receive abundance of grace and of the gift of righteousness will reign in life through the one, Jesus Christ." It says you will reign in life. You are an "overcomer." If you are not experiencing victory, it is a breech of the Word of God. Command the circumstances to leave and take hold of the victory that is yours through the Word. For this is the will of God!

Colossians 1:13 (nkjv) says, "He has delivered us from the power of darkness and conveyed us into the kingdom of the Son of His love." To be conveyed is to be transferred—moved out of one place and into another. The power of darkness that includes the curse no longer has a hold on us as we are now members of a different kingdom—the kingdom of God! There is no disease and no sickness in the kingdom of God.

Jesus is Lord so Close All Doors to the Enemy!
Proverbs 3:7-8 (NKJV) says, "Do not be wise in your own eyes; fear the Lord and depart from evil. It will be health to your flesh, and strength to your bones." "Fear the Lord" means to revere the Lord and worship the Lord in all things.

> If thou will diligently heed to the voice of the Lord your God, and wilt do that which is right in His sight, and wilt give ear to His commandments, and keep all his statutes, I will put (permit) none of these diseases upon thee, which I have brought upon the Egyptians: for I am the Lord that heals you.
>
> Exodus 15:26 (NKJV)

Exodus 23:25 (NKJV) says, "So you shall serve the Lord your God and He will bless your bread and your water. And He will take sickness away from the midst of you." Divine health is found in worshiping the Lord. Follow Him!

Psalms 91:9-10 (KJV) says, "Because you have made the Lord, which is my refuge, even the Most High, your dwelling place, no evil shall befall you, nor shall any plague come near your dwelling."

Malachi 4:2-3 (NKJV) says, "But unto you that fear (worship) My name the Sun of Righteousness shall arise with healing in his wings; you shall go out and grow fat like stall-fed calves. You shall trample the wicked, for they shall be ashes under the soles of your feet on the day that I do this," says the Lord of hosts. "On the day that I do this" was at Calvary. Now the enemy is "ashes" under our feet and healing and protection belong to us.

Know that when you ask the Lord for healing, it is His will. He hears you and agrees. He has settled it in the atonement of the blood of Jesus Christ—He says, "Yes!"

Psalm 30:2 (KJV) says, "O Lord my God, I cry unto thee, and thou hast healed me."

Psalm 107:19-20 (KJV) says, "Then they cry unto the Lord in their trouble, and He saves them out of their distresses. He sent His Word, and healed them, and delivered them from their destructions."

Matthew 7:7-8 (KJV) says, "Ask, and it will be given to you; seek, and you will find; knock, and it will be opened to you. For everyone who asks receives, and he who seeks finds, and to him who knocks it will be opened,"

1 John 5:14-15 (NKJV) says, "Now this is the confidence we have in Him, that if we ask anything according to His will, He hears us. And if we know that He hears us, whatever we ask, we know that we have the petitions that we have asked of Him." The Word of God is the will of God. If you see it in the Word of God, then you can be assured

that it is the will of God. The Lord is not trying to keep healing from you; He is trying to get it *to* you. Just believe!

2 Corinthians 1:20 (NKJV) says, "For all the promises of God in Him are Yes, and in Him Amen, to the glory of God through us." According to God, all of His promises toward us are "Yes" and "Amen" (so be it!). There are no "nos" from the Lord to us when it comes to performing His Word.

Psalm 35:27 (NKJV) says, "Let them shout for joy and be glad, who favor my righteous cause; and let them say continually, Let the Lord be magnified, who has pleasure in the prosperity of His servant." The word in Hebrew for prosperity is "shalom." This word literally means health, prosperity, and peace-wholeness, welfare. So you can clearly see the mind of God who takes pleasure in the health, wholeness, prosperity, and peace of us His children!

He loves us so much. Praise God!

God's Word Brings Healing!

Psalm 119:50 (NKJV) says, "This is my comfort in my affliction, For your word has given me life."

Romans 10:17 (NKJV) says, "So then faith comes by hearing and hearing by the Word of God." Faith for healing comes by hearing God's Word concerning healing. Just as you may be taking medicine two or three times a day, do the same thing with the promises in the Word of God regarding healing and allow your faith to grow!

Proverbs 4:20-22 (NKJV) says, "My Son, give attention to my words; incline your ear to my sayings. Do not let them depart from your eyes; keep them in the midst of your heart; for they are life to those who find them, and health to all their flesh." Here it is as plain as it can be; the taking of God's Word is health to your flesh.

John 8:32 (NKJV) says, "And you shall know the truth, and the truth shall set you free." The Word of God is truth and once you know the truth concerning healing you can begin to exercise faith and expect the promises of God to manifest in you. You will be set free of the curse. You will be healed!

2 Timothy 3:16-17 (NKJV) says, "All Scripture is given by inspiration of God, and is profitable for doctrine, for reproof, for correction, for instruction in righteousness, that the man of God may be complete, thoroughly equipped for every good work." God's Word is like medicine that you may be complete and thoroughly equipped for every good work. If you are sick, you cannot do the work of the ministry. God wants you to be strong and able-bodied—a living example in every area of His grace and mercy and power.

John 6:63 (NKJV) says, "It is the spirit who gives life; the flesh profits nothing. The words that I speak to you are spirit, and they are life." God's Word is healing. It brings health to your spirit, mind, and body. That is why it is important to go over the healing scriptures daily, building your faith in the area of healing, imparting to you the very life of God!

John 15:7 (NKJV) says, "If you abide in Me, and My words abide in you, you will ask what you desire, and it shall be done for you."

Isaiah 55:11 (NKJV) says, "So shall My word be that goes forth from My mouth; it shall not return to Me void, but it shall accomplish what I please, and it shall prosper in the thing for which I sent it." God's Word on healing will heal you!

Jeremiah 1:12 (AMP) says, "…I am alert and active watching over My word to perform it." God is looking for someone to take Him at His Word so he can perform it on their behalf.

Joshua 21:45 (NKJV) says, "Not a word failed of any good thing which the Lord had spoken to the house of Israel. All came to pass." How much more sure is this promise to us since it is based on the new covenant in Christ?

Healing Is a Good Gift from God!

James 1:17 (NKJV) says, "Every good gift and every perfect gift is from above, and comes down from the Father of lights, with whom there is no variation or shadow of turning." Healing is a wonderful gift from God. This is another proof from His Word that He does not change. Praise the Lord! What He did yesterday He will do again today; He is still the Lord that heals!

1 Corinthians 3:21-22 (NKJV) says, "Therefore let no one boast in men. For all things are yours: whether Paul or Apollos or Cephas, or the world or life or death, or things present or things to come-all are yours." The Lord is holding nothing back from us. Begin to praise him for your healing and the manifestation will come as you receive the promise of faith.

Romans 11:29 (NKJV) says, "For the gifts and the calling of God are irrevocable." He's the giver of gifts. He doesn't take them back.

Phillipians 2:13 (NKJV) says, "For it is God who works in you both to will and to do for His good pleasure."

Matthew 11:28 (NKJV) says, "Come to Me, all you who labor and are heavy laden, and I will give you rest." The word "rest" means to cease from toil or labor in order to recover and collect strength. It implies a feeling of wholeness and well being. Place your focus on Jesus and all He has done for you. Take the focus off the problems and praise God for all that he has done for you. You are highly favored by God. Spend time each day in intimate worship just loving him. You will experience His "rest."

We Have Been Redeemed from the Bondage of Sickness and Disease!

Galatians 3:13-14 (NKJV) says, "Christ has redeemed us from the curse of the law, being made a curse for us; for it is written, cursed is every one that hangs on a tree: That the blessings of Abraham might come on the Gentiles through Jesus Christ." The curse of the law includes sickness and disease. By Jesus's blood we were freed from the curse.

Proverbs 26:2 (NKJV) says, "Like a flitting sparrow, like a flying swallow, so a curse without cause shall not alight." As we continue in Christ and as we stay God-centered the curse has no right to take root in our lives. Take a firm stand against it. Command its effects to leave in the name of Jesus. You are a child of the King.

Romans 8:2 (NKJV) says, "For the law of the spirit of life in Christ Jesus has made me free from the law of sin and death."

Colossians 1:13 (NKJV) says, "He has delivered us from the power of darkness and conveyed us into the kingdom of the Son of His Love." Remember, there is no sickness or disease in God's kingdom. It is your birthright to be healed!

1 John 3:8b (NKJV) says, "For this purpose the Son of God was manifested, that he might destroy the works of the devil." This is translated in the Amplified version as, "The reason the Son of God was made manifest (visible) was to undo (destroy, loosen, and dissolve) the works of the devil." Sickness and disease is the work of the devil, introduced to mankind through the fall as part of the curse. This scripture is clear. Jesus came to undue the work of the devil. Sickness and disease have no legal right to remain in your body. Command it to go in Jesus's name!

John 8:35 (NKJV) says, "Therefore if the Son makes you free, you shall be free indeed." Let this truth soak deep into your heart. It will dispel all thoughts of doubt and fear. Praise God that sickness and disease cannot stay; they have to go! Jesus overcame the curse.

Snap Out of that Depression— Your Attitude Determines Your Altitude!

Hebrews 12:12-13 (KJV) says, "Wherefore lift up the hands which hang down, and the feeble knees; and make straight paths for your feet, lest that which is lame be turned out of the way; but let it rather be healed." Faith rejoices at the promises of God. Get your focus off of the problem and onto the answer found in the promises of God. Rejoice! Get happy! Nehemiah 8:10b (NKJV) "The joy of the Lord is your strength."

Psalm 42:11 (NKJV) says, "Why are you cast down, O my soul? And why are you disquieted within me? Hope in God; for I shall yet praise Him, the help of my countenance and my God."

Have Confidence in Him—God Cannot Lie!

Hebrew 10:23 (KJV) says, "Let us hold fast the profession of our faith without wavering; (for he is faithful that promised)." Remember, Hebrews 6:18 says that it is impossible for God to lie!

1 John 5:14-15 (NKJV) says, "Now this is the confidence that we have in Him, that if we ask anything according to His will, He hears us. And if we know that he hears us, whatever we ask, we know that we have the petitions that we have asked of Him," The Word of God is the will of God! Jeremiah 1:12 (AMP) says that He watches over His Word to perform it. God's will be done! He will fulfill His Word.

Hebrews 10:35-36 (NKJV) says, "Therefore do not cast away your confidence, which has great reward. For you have need of endurance, so that after you have done the will of God, you may receive the promise." Live a God-centered life, and His glory will manifest!

Base Your Faith on God's Promises— Long Life Belongs to You!

Job 5:26 (NKJV) says, "You shall come to the grave at a full age, as a sheaf of grain ripens in its season."

Psalm 91:16 (NKJV) says, "With long life I will satisfy him, and show him My Salvation."

Psalm 118:17 (NKJV) says, "I shall not die, but live, and declare the works of the Lord." Confess it with your voice. God has a plan for your life. Don't let the enemy steal your victory! Cast down thoughts and imaginations that are not consistent with the Word of God!

> (For the weapons of our warfare are not carnal, but mighty through God to the pulling down of strongholds;) Casting down imaginations, and every high thing that exalts itself against the knowledge of God, and bringing into captivity every thought of the obedience to Christ.
>
> 2 Corinthians 10:4-5 (KJV)

Keep your focus on the promises of God. Stay focused on God's truth. Don't listen to Satan's lies. Your healing is on it's way! State your case to God!

Isaiah 43:25-26 (KJV) says, "I, even I, am He who blots out your transgressions for My own sake; and I will not remember your sins. Put Me in remembrance; let us contend together; state your case, that you may be acquitted." If you have accepted Jesus Christ as your Savior, then "It is finished." Stay God-centered!

Your Words are Important and Powerful!
Isaiah 57:19 (KJV) says, "I create the fruit of the lips; Peace, peace be to him that is far off, and to him that is near, says the Lord; and I will heal him." When we believe and speak the Word of God, He creates what we speak. There is power in our confessions.

> And Jesus answering said unto them, have faith in God. For verily I say unto you, that whosoever says to this mountain, 'Be removed and be cast into the sea' and does not doubt in his heart, but believes that those things he says will be done, he will have whatever he says.
>
> Mark 11:22-23 (KJV)

Mountains come in many forms. Command your mountain of pain, cancer, and disease to go now in the name of Jesus. Jesus said you can have what you confess. Begin to confess your body to be whole-healed and well.

Listen to Jesus...Not Your Body!

> For then you will delight in the Almighty, and lift up your face to God. You will pray to Him, and He will hear you; and you will pay your vows. You will also declare a thing, and it will be established for you; and the light will shine on your ways.
>
> Job 22:26-28 (NKJV)

Confess the promises in the word. Claim them as your inheritance. Lord, your word says that by your stripes I am healed. So, on the authority of your Word, I claim that I am healed. Sickness and disease have no hold on me, and they must go in the name of Jesus! I am free of the curse!

Give Testimony of Your Healing!

Revelation 12:11 (KJV) says, "And they overcame him by the blood of the lamb, and by the word of their testimony..."

When you recover and have the opportunity to testify to the grace of the Lord, do it! The Lord wants you to give glory to Him for what He has done. Your testimony will serve to help build faith in others who have needs.

Hold On to Your Healing!

Nahum 1:7-9b (KJV) says, "The Lord is good, a stronghold in the day of trouble; and He knows those who trust in Him…He will make an utter end of it. Affliction will not rise up a second time."

We have established the scriptural foundation for believing God for your healing. We have established your authority over sickness and disease that is found in Christ Jesus. You must resist fear. You are an overcomer through Jesus. You must make Jesus the Lord of your life. Then you know that when you ask the Lord for healing that it is His will. The Lord hears you and agrees. You know that he has already settled it in the atonement of the blood of Jesus. He says "yes." The Word of God brings healing. Healing is a gift from God. We have been redeemed from the bondage of sickness and disease so keep a positive attitude and have confidence in God—for He cannot lie. Long life belongs to you. Do not give up! Base your faith on God's promises. Cast down those thoughts and imaginations that don't line up with the Word of God. State your case to God remembering that your words are important. Remember to give testimony of your healing and hold on to your healing.

Action step—Please dwell on these scriptures daily to fill your spirit, soul, and body with these seeds of God's truth. It is my hope and prayer that your faith will grow and God's promise will manifest in your life. Your prayers will be answered, and you will be healed.

While supplies last you may receive the CD, "Healing Scriptures" narrated by Dr. Gary Coller for a donation of $10.00 to Cathedral of Glory Ministries. Contact us at 616-772-0700.

Building Faith

Overcome Doubt

Scripture describes failures in healing as a lack of faith. According to Matthew 13:58, (NASB) "He did not do many miracles there because of their unbelief." They did not come to Jesus for help because they did not believe in Him. When the disciples asked Jesus why they could not heal a boy in Matthew 17:19b-21 (AMP), Jesus said to them, "Because of the littleness of your faith [that is, lack of firmly relying trust] For truly I say to you, if you have faith [that is living] like a grain of mustard seed, you will say to this mountain, move from here to yonder place, and it will move, and nothing will be impossible to you. But this kind does not go out except by prayer and fasting." Jesus revealed that they failed to help the boy because their faith was not energized by fasting and prayer. They were unprepared to deal with the boy's situation. So again I encourage you build your faith by listening to the "Healing Scriptures." Humble yourself and recognize that you might need additional preparation. 1 Thessalonians 3:10 encourages us to keep praying day and night and pray earnestly to see God's face that He would complete what is lacking in your faith. Then energize your faith with fasting. Remember, our lack of faith is not a problem with God. It is a problem with us. Keep pressing in.

Please, please, please don't get hung up on legalistic requirements and conditions for healing. Anything more than simple faith in Christ for healing creates doubt. When we start to question that the healing has not occurred because of un-forgiveness, lack of tithing, not giving enough, not submitting, not attending church, watching the wrong movie, etc…our faith dies. Focus only on doing those things that build faith…prayer, fasting, and getting into the Word of God.

After Peter attempted to walk on the water, Jesus asked in Matthew 14:31 (AMP), "O you of little faith, why did you doubt?" Peter had taken his eyes off of Jesus. He began to focus on the storm. He began to doubt. His faith faded. He began to sink. Don't focus on the negatives! Don't focus on the "what ifs." Don't focus on failure. Focus on the victory in Christ. By His stripes you were healed! Accept your healing!

No earthbound human relationship or religious act is required for healing from a spiritual perspective. Just come to Jesus in simple faith.

As we have previously discussed, it may be necessary to become more God-centered. The negative emotions of the self-centered life may leave us feeling unworthy to come before God's throne to ask for a healing. We may be saved and washed in the blood of Jesus, yet our soul (conscience) condemns us and makes us feel unworthy. If and when this happens it may be necessary to rectify issues and eliminate the blocking emotions to manifesting God's will through our souls to our body. By rejecting error in our lives we are able to come before God's throne and receive healing. Again, it is God's will to heal you. Jesus has done it all. Just come to Jesus in simple faith.

Fasting

We have discussed the development of an intensely personal relationship with Jesus based on His sacrifice and His Word. That intimate relationship results in our being healed spirit, soul, and body. Jesus dealt with it all. His sacrifice was sufficient. As we worship Him in spirit and in truth His will becomes manifest in our lives. That includes His will to heal us.

Key to health—Remembering God's benefits

> Bless the Lord, O my soul, and forget not all His benefits, who forgives all your iniquities, who heals all your diseases. Who redeems your life from destruction, who crowns you with loving kindness and tender mercies, who satisfies your mouth with good things, so that your youth is renewed like the eagle's.
>
> Psalm 103:2-5 (Lamsa)

That intimate relationship can be hindered when we get caught up in the cares of this world. Fasting is a means of detaching ourselves from the material so that our thinking becomes focused on God and the unseen world of which He is the center. This results in increased faith, which is "The assurance of things hoped for, the conviction of things not seen" (Hebrews 11:1 AVS).

It is often the case that the quickening of faith brought on by fasting results in God supernaturally fulfilling his promise of healing.

There are also natural healing and rejuvenating forces at work when we fast. Disease is often the result of overabundant living without restraint. The Edwin Smith Papyrus quotes an Egyptian doctor 3,700 years ago saying, "Man eats too much. Thus, he lives on only a quarter of what he consumes. The doctor, however, lives on the remaining three quarters."[9]

We might say that there is nothing new under the sun. Overeating coupled with poor nutritional choices has resulted in a myriad of well documented health issues. Degenerative joint disease, attention deficit disorder, adult onset diabetes, hyperlipidemia, coronary disease, hardening of the arteries, cancer, and many more maladies can be directly linked to what we consume. Therefore, it can only help to periodically purge our bodies of excess with fasting. During a fast the body purges itself of fat stores, waste materials, and the decaying tissues are being digested and eliminated.

During a fast the body does not have to deal with assimilating food. Instead, it directs the energy to elimination and the body naturally detoxifies!

Think of fasting as rebooting your computer. Now that you are up and running again, be careful what you download. A computer responds to the information we put into it. Our spirit, soul, and body are also responsive to how they are fed. Put good in and you get good results. Put bad in and you decay.

Fasting can be healthy both spiritually and physically. Please do not partake of a fast, though, without proper medical supervision.

Action step—I recommend that you obtain and read *God's Chosen Fast*, which is a spiritual and practical guide to fasting by Arthur Wallis. When coming off your fast, I would also recommend ideas from Jordan Rubin's book *The Maker's Diet*. This book has practical ideas leading you to proper nutrition, natural detoxification, and for reaching and maintaining optimal health.

Speak God's Truth

One of the most important principles to divine health and healing is speaking God's truth. If God said it, believe it and confess it. There is great power in your confessions (the words you speak).

God called Abram "the father of many nations" before he had the promised child. Despite his advanced age, God changed Abrams name to Abraham (meaning father of nations). Through this, God taught Abraham to call for what he did not yet have. God gave a promise. As Abram confessed his name, "Abraham," he called for the reality of God's promise to be manifest. Romans 4:17-22 (KJV) says, "(As it is written, I have made the father of many nations,) before him whom he believed, even God who quickeneth the dead and calleth those things which be not as though they were." Abraham did not go around denying his age. He was old. By declaring "I am Abraham," (father of nations) he was mixing his faith with God's Word until the confession became manifest in reality.

This principle is further established in 1 Corinthians 1:27, 28 (KJV)

> But God hath chosen the foolish things of the world to confound the wise; and God hath chosen the weak things of the world to confound the things which are mighty; and base things of the world, and things which are despised, hath God chosen, yea,

> and things which are not to bring to naught things that are.

This tells us that God uses spiritual forces (the unseen) to nullify natural things (that are seen). This is the Bible principle of speaking God's truth or calling things that are not as though they are.

2 Corinthians 4:13 (KJV) advances this thought. "We having the same spirit of faith, according as it is written, I believe and therefore have I spoken; we also believe, and therefore speak."

This principle is vitally important if we want to obtain divine healing. We must declare, over ourselves, the truths that God's Word reveals about us. Our confessions cannot be based on how we feel or our current circumstances. Our confessions must line up with God's Word.

Romans 10:8 (KJV) established "…the word is nigh thee, even in thy mouth and in thy heart." The Word is first in your mouth, and then it progresses to your heart. As you confess God's truth, the seed is planted within you until you "own it" and your faith grows. Speaking God's Word is a means of calling God's promises to manifest in our lives.

You are not denying reality. You are not denying that a sickness exists. You are denying its right to exist in your body. You have every right to do this because you have been redeemed from the cause of the law and delivered from the authority of darkness (Galatians 3:13 and Colossians 1:13, KJV).

2 Peter 1:3-4 (KJV) tells us that God has given you all things that pertain to life and Godliness. If or when you are sick, you have every right to confess God's Word that you were (are) healed by the stripes of Jesus. You are confessing (calling out for) what God has already given you in His Word even though it is not yet manifest in your life.

There is no power in merely denying that sickness exists. The power is in confessing health and healing by mixing faith and God's Word. In this way, you are calling God's Word to be manifest in your body.

As your faith builds, healing occurs. As you confess your body is healed, according to Luke 17:5-6 (KJV) and Mark 11:23 (KJV), "Your body is listening and it will obey if you believe and don't doubt in your heart."

The converse is also true…so be careful what you confess!

Statements like "you make me sick" should be avoided at all cost.

Action step—A trick I learned to help control my tongue is to put a rubber band around my wrist. Each time I find myself making an inappropriate remark, I pull on the rubber band to inflict a small pain as it snaps back. Try this. In a short time, you will become more tuned into your words. It may greatly change your life!

Natural Aging

The Mighty River of God
In these pages, I have equated fear with being a product of a self-centered life. There is, though, a healthy and necessary fear. The fear of the Lord is the beginning of wisdom. Staying in the will of God is like floating down a river; the more we fight the current of God's will, the more we are buffeted by the force of the stream. It is to our peril if we fight the stream of God's will in our lives. Fear God and stay in His perfect will. When we fight the stream of God's will we move our vessel [our lives] into places God wants us to avoid.

Using this analogy, let's review what we have learned. God's will is the stream directing us toward His purposes. "I wish above all things that thou mayest prosper and be in health, even as the soul prospereth" (3 John 1:2, KJV). We know, then, that it is God's will to carry us down this river to health, prosperity, and the fruits of a God centered life. Until it is our time to leave and be with the Lord in heaven, it is God's will that we float down the river of His will toward health and healing.

We have seen that in moving away from the God-centered life into the self-centered life, we become buffeted by negative forces. If we repent and turn back into the will of God, he is faithful to forgive. We will again be flowing to health, healing, prosperity, etc.

Key to health—Obeying the voice of God

> And he said to him, If you will diligently harken to the voice of the Lord your God and will do that which is right in His sight and will obey His commandments and keep all His statutes, I will bring none of these plagues upon you which I have brought upon the Egyptians; for I am the Lord your healer.
>
> Exodus 15:26 (Lamsa)

> ...say to them, As I live, says the Lord God, I do not desire the death of the wicked; but that the wicked should turn from his evil ways and live.
>
> Ezekiel 33:11 (Lamsa)

Then there are times when, due to forces seemingly out of our control, a big wave comes along and capsizes our vessel. We need help, and we need it now. Remember, we are in a spiritual battle, and sometimes Satan wants to rock our boat. We have seen, though, that "greater is He that is in you than he that is in the world" (1 John 4:4, KJV). That is, Jesus dwells within believers, and Jesus is greater than Satan—the prince of this self-centered materialistic world.

So when our boat capsizes, we call out to God. We have faith. As we keep our eyes fixed on God, He rights our vessel and directs us out of harm's way. Some might call it a miracle. It is our loving God's will for you. He says in John 14:6 (KJV), "I am the way, the truth, and the life." Keep your vessel God-centered and everything will work together for good because you will stay in His perfect will.

Key to health—Having faith and not giving up

Let us not be weary in well doing; for in due season we shall reap, if we faint not.

Galatians 6:9 (Lamsa)

And that you be not slothful, but be followers of those who through faith and patience have become heirs of the promise.

Hebrews 6:12 (Lamsa)

Do not lose, therefore, the confidence that you have, for it has a great reward. For you have need of patience in order that you may do the will of God and receive the promise.

Hebrews 10:35-36 (Lamsa)

As we float along this stream being navigated by our Lord Jesus, we can still develop problems. If we indulge in over-abundant living without restraints, our body can become burdened with excess fat and toxins. Becoming more disciplined (eating right, exercising, and controlled fasting) can go a long way toward detoxifying and purifying your body. Being more disciplined and fasting not only benefits the body, but it also helps the spirit to better focus on God. The closer we are focused on God, the more we experience his awesome presence…How wonderful it is to bask in his presence…The mighty river of God is filled with passion, truth, glory, and grace…Oh, what rest.

Then we wake up and realize that we are not in the Garden of Eden any longer…Horns blaring, children sneezing, the boss is demanding, oh, and that smog. Pollution is everywhere. We can't avoid all the germs… the worst of the killer germs seem to be in hospitals. Then there are parasites, bomb threats, radiation exposure, drug interactions, and side effects. What kind of a nightmare did we wake up to?

We thought we had our life straight, yet there are people sinning all around us. And even though we act Christlike to those around us, there are actually people taking advantage of us. "It just isn't fair. It just isn't right," we say in frustration.

How quickly the world can pull us away from our place of peace with God. When this happens, repent, turn back to God as quickly as possible, and ask him to forgive you for your wrong attitude. In all things, pray, praise, and give thanks.

Once you get yourself God-centered again, you take inventory. You are beginning to realize that, despite your best efforts, life is slowly taking its toll on your vessel. As a matter of fact, when you look closely, your vessel is getting nicked up. Life takes its toll, and as we live our vessel ages.

Many of the nicks heal quickly. More serious damage may require interventions. Never limit the means by which God will repair your vessel. God is sovereign. He does not always function in the miraculous.

Action step—Seek first the kingdom of God and all else will be added unto you. You may be healed by getting rid of negative emotions. You may be healed "miraculously" by faith or God may have another idea!

When we try to hear God's ideas, it can be difficult. If you have read the book *Men are from Mars, Women are from Venus* by John Gray, PhD, you will understand that, generally speaking, there are differences between Martians and Venusians. They look at things differently. They communicate differently. They understand things differently. They have different needs and ways of dealing with life. Well, God is from heaven, and we are from the third rock from the sun (Earth). God is spirit. He communicates through the spirit. We are earthly beings. The more earthly-minded we are, the more rock-headed we become.

As we stop focusing our minds on the material earthly existence, we start to hear the still voice in our spirit.

God has tried to communicate with us by giving us His Son. His love language to us was in the passion of Christ (His death and resurrection) that we might have eternal life with Him. He gave us His Holy Spirit to live within us and direct our lives.

Try to see things from the perspective that God loves you. He is on your side. Remember, we may be having difficulty understanding His language. His ways are higher than our ways.

A child does not always understand the love that their parents feel toward them. The child may be angry because they want more candy. The parent knows that more candy will harm the child. The parent must give tough love for the child's well being. If these misunderstandings happen often enough, the parent and child develop distrust and become estranged from each other.

The same thing can happen between you and God. If that has happened to you, try to make a paradigm shift. Assume He loves you. Assume He has good motives…not bad ones. Let Him love you. That is His desire. Turn to Him. Love Him. Stop thinking in terms of "What's in it for me?" It's all about God. The "I am" is within us. The "I am" is Jesus!

Some Important Functional Medicine Concepts

In a great flood, they worked their way to the roof of their house. "God, rescue me," they prayed. Soon, a rowboat came by but they refused to get into the boat. Instead, they would wait for God to rescue them. The water continued to rise, and they continued to pray for God to rescue them.

A bit later, a helicopter came by and dropped a basket on a line. "Get in," the pilot yelled.

Again, they refused. "God will rescue us!" they screamed. But instead, they drowned. "God why didn't you rescue us?" they asked.

God replied, "What did you want from me? I sent a boat *and* a helicopter!"

Don't require God to act a certain way. Don't tempt God to perform a miracle. Sometimes, he gives us knowledge and the means to rescue ourselves. He has set certain laws in force that will naturally lead to healing. Going against those laws can be disastrous.

God gave us brains. He wants us to use them. Put Him first. Listen to what He says. Do what He tells you. God wants us to be involved. We are his hands and feet. He works through us.

As I discussed earlier, we do not live in the Garden of Eden. This is not paradise. We have all kinds of pollution. We have discussed this from a spiritual perspective acknowledging the physical consequences of negative emotions and a self-centered, sin-filled existence. Now let's focus on subjecting our bodies to other pollution…heavy toxic metals, antibiotics, steroids, foods filled with empty calories, trans fats, too much sugar, refined carbohydrates in the diet, not enough water, too much alcohol, too much caffeine, parasites, bacteria, and on and on and on.

Traditional medicine with drugs and surgery is wonderful but limited by its own structure. New diseases are often unexplained symptom complexes. Research money is given to find a means of altering these symptom complexes. The system rewards those who come up with a drug or immunization that will change the symptoms. It is especially helpful if we can attribute the symptoms to something that is provoking of fear…killer virus, genetic anomaly, etc. This is well and good, but the result of continually walking this path is that we become very short sighted. We begin accepting therapies that make us feel better today but lead to us decaying more quickly tomorrow. You exchange arthritic pain today for a heart attack tomorrow. What happens when you mix remedies? With thousands of drugs and new ones developed regularly, the chemical combinations being put into our bodies is endless! These combinations have not been adequately studied!

Other than in an emergency, surgery should be avoided due to well-documented toxicity of anesthesia, scar tissue, morbidity, and mortality. So whenever possible try to avoid surgery and drugs. Let's review a more common sense approach to health and healing.

Over the years, I have encountered hundreds of patients telling me, in effect, that they have been to twenty doctors. They tried everything and nothing worked. The symptoms persisted, so the doctors said it must be in their head. It is often the position of "traditional medicine" that if the remedy doesn't work, its not the fault of the medical approach…it is the fault of the patient. The patient will go on to say that they can't take it anymore. "Doc, you are my last resort. If this doesn't work, I'll kill myself."

I praise God for the many lives that have been saved using a common sense approach. Sometimes medicine is so busy looking at disease through complicated formulas and self-protective eyewear that it fails to step back and see the big picture. They forget to see the forest because they are focused so narrowly on the trees.

So let's step back and view examples of the bigger picture. We find that when we care for the forest many of the trees take care of themselves.

Hippocrates is quoted to have said that health starts with the intestine. The reason for this is the small intestine is where we assimilate the nutrients from the food that is broken down in the stomach.

Adequate amounts of digestive enzymes and stomach acid are necessary for this breakdown to occur.

For various reasons, people take antacids. When they do this, they neutralize the acidity in the stomach. The more alkaline the stomach acids become, the more difficult it will be to digest food. This can make food stagnate and putrefy, causing gas and pressure in the stomach leading to gastro esophageal reflux (GERD) and bloating. These conditions were probably the reason the antacid was used initially. As we get older, the levels of stomach acid tend to decrease—not increase. It takes a lot of energy for the body to turn water into acid for digestion. (Note that acidity in the stomach is very different from the body tissues becoming acidic due to toxic build up).

Action step—If you have trouble with digestion, ask your doctor to get a Heidelberg test on you. This test actually measures the acidity in the stomach. You might also consider a comprehensive digestive stool analysis to determine your need for digestive enzymes.

Now that you are breaking your food down for absorption, it dumps into the small intestine. It is very important that the digestive tract be nourished with adequate B-12. Without the intrinsic factor found in B-12, the absorption of nutrients will be hindered. The Cochran Foundation has discovered that one of the most important problems leading to aging involves our inability to assimilate, store, and utilize amino acids. Approximately 75 percent of the body's dry weight is amino acids. Proteins that we ingest are broken down in the stomach to amino acids. Our ability to absorb and assimilate them into our bodies is key to health because the amino acids are key to chemical reactions necessary for life.

Tim Cochran, the chief biochemist at the Cochran Foundation, has determined that we start life with a certain ability to assimilate amino acids. That ability usually increases from birth to the early twenties, levels off for two or three years, and then starts a slow process of decline until our amino acids have reached a critical level. We can no longer carry out essential chemical reaction, so we become diseased. Negative genetic expressions are manifest.

Amino Acid Assimilation

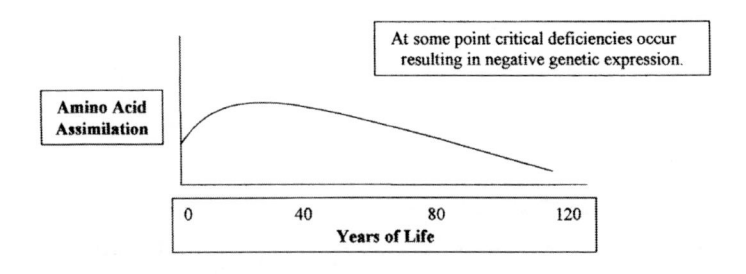

At some point critical deficiencies occur resulting in negative genetic expression.

0   40   80   120
Years of Life

An example of this is Parkinson's disease. Without the assimilation of specific amino acids the body cannot produce glutathione. Glutathione is a neurotransmitter in the brain. It is also a detoxifier of the liver and the brain. When glutathione becomes deficient toxins accumulate in the substantia nigra of the brain. This blocks dopamine production. This results in Parkinson's. Similar patterns exist for many other medical conditions.

It is interesting that many of the drugs used to treat Parkinson's are thought to increase the toxic build up and aggravate the condition. Therefore, many times we see that the Parkinson's symptoms are better with the use of the meds…but the patient actually deteriorates more rapidly because the medications were used.

Action step—You can assess amino acids with a fasting amino acid assay.

Similarly, fatty acids are very important to a person's health and well being. As an example, our brains are composed, in large part, of fat. There are good and bad fats, cis- and trans- fats, non-inflammatory and inflammatory fats, as well as essential and non-essential fatty acids. A proper balance of fats is essential in the treatment of neurological disorders like Parkinson's, Alzheimer's, Autism, Aspergers, Attention Deficit, Hyperactivity, and many others. Proper balance of fatty acids is essential to cardiovascular health, as well. We now know that 85 percent of fatal heart attacks are caused by inflammation in the lining of the coronary arteries. The artery cracks and releases clotting factors associated with the "vulnerable plaque." "Vulnerable plaque" is young plaque that has not completely hardened. It is still somewhat liquid. It is located in the wall of the artery. If the inflamed artery ruptures, the clotting cascade is triggered by the plaque material. This results in a clot and causes occlusion of blood flow. Lack of blood flow deprives the heart of oxygen, the tissue dies, and there you have a heart attack!

Action step—You can assess the balance of fats in your body with a fasting fatty acid analysis. You can assess for inflammation in the blood vessels with the cardiac CRP test (The ultra sensitive c reactive protein test).

A high triglyceride level impacts vulnerable plaque in a very dangerous way. High triglyceride levels cause hypoxia (lack of oxygen). The hypoxia converts macrophages into triglyceride laden foam cells. The foam cells create inflammation. The inflammation causes the vulnerable plaque to rupture. When the vulnerable plaque ruptures, clotting factors are released, clots form, and arterial occlusion occurs.

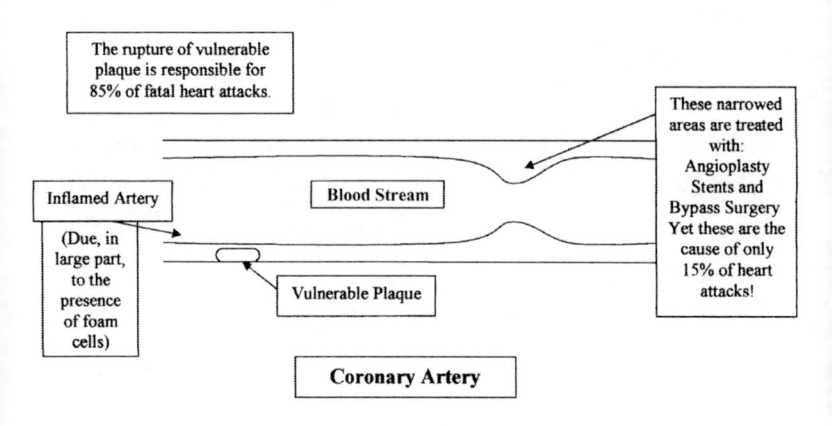

The rupture of vulnerable plaque is responsible for 85% of fatal heart attacks.

These narrowed areas are treated with: Angioplasty Stents and Bypass Surgery Yet these are the cause of only 15% of heart attacks!

Inflamed Artery (Due, in large part, to the presence of foam cells)

Blood Stream

Vulnerable Plaque

Coronary Artery

Action step—This is one of the many reasons it is important to take your antioxidants. The antioxidants help prevent the oxidation of the triglycerides. Taking antioxidants can reduce the formation of "foam cells" and minimize the risk of heart attack.

The reason so many of us have problems with high triglyceride levels is that we eat too much. We consume incredible amounts of sugar and processed foods. These foods raise your blood sugar quickly. The high blood sugar demands the body to respond by the pancreas producing insulin. Insulin lowers the blood sugar by converting it into free fatty acids. The excess free fatty acids cause an elevation in triglycerides. It also causes a person to gain weight.

If this happens over a long period of time, the body will become depleted of mineral cofactors such as chromium and vanadium. These are necessary for insulin to do its job. Without the mineral cofactors, insulin levels go up, but the sugar stays high, also. You develop insulin resistance. This can ultimately lead to adult onset diabetes.

Action step—Consider limiting your intake of foods that raise your blood sugar quickly. Eat fresh whole foods with a low glycemic index. Avoid things that irritate your pancreas, such as processed foods, sugar, alcohol, and caffeine.

As blood sugar levels become imbalanced, the stage is set for yeast to begin to grow out of control in the intestine…then spread throughout the rest of the body! It is normal to have a small amount of yeast in the digestive tract. Yeast overgrowth is controlled by beneficial bacteria, such as acidophilus and bifidus, that are also found in the intestine. Taking antibiotics and/or being exposed to heavy metals and other toxic substances may kill the beneficial bacteria and yeast can grow unrestrained.

This sets the stage for yeast infections throughout the body…vaginal candida, jock itch, thrush, tinea unguium, tinea corporus, etc.

Action step—If you use an antibiotic, always replenish your bowel with a good probiotic (acidophilus and bifidus). Consider a comprehensive digestive stool analysis to assess for the presence of good bacteria and for an overabundance of yeast.

Each individual yeast has a life cycle. When it dies, it gives off a toxin—an aldehyde. If that toxin goes to the brain, it can cause confusion, irritability, light-headedness, and dizziness. It is a major cause of fatigue. If it goes to the gut, it can cause bloating, gas, diarrhea, and constipation. Also, in the gut, it has a direct effect on the intestinal lining. It causes the cells of the intestinal lining to atrophy. As you lose the integrity of the lining of your intestine, it becomes permeable to larger particles. You start absorbing larger particles across the intestine and back into your blood stream. You start reabsorbing your stool back into your body! This is referred to as "Leaky Gut." Most people by age forty seem to have some degree of this problem.

Action step—A simple lactulose/mannitol test can evaluate you for Leaky Gut.

As bad as "Leaky Gut" may sound, when you first develop it, you probably won't even notice. This is because we have a secondary defense. We have substances including glutathione, glutamic acid, glycine, cysteine and sulfa that package these toxins to remove them through the liver and kidneys. In general, the fat soluble toxins go out through the liver. Water soluble toxins are excreted through the kidneys.

It is after you bombard the system too aggressively for too long that it becomes overwhelmed and you become acidic. The body then goes into its third line of defense. It utilizes oxygen to neutralize the toxins. Your tissues become more acidic. This leads to oxidative stress: inflammation, degenerative disease, arthritis, hardening of the arteries, Parkinson's, Alzheimer's, memory loss, cancer, etc. If you don't keep your carburetor or gas filter clean, your car engine sputters and shuts down. So, too, does your bodily system struggle once it gets "gummed up."

As the fat soluble toxins increase, the bile becomes thicker. When the bile dumps from the liver to the gallbladder and into the small intestine, it is supposed to mix into your stool and pass out of the body. The thickened bile does not easily mix into the stool and will begin to be reabsorbed into the body. This is referred to as enterohepatic reabsorption of toxins. This compounds the problem. Cholesterol and fat soluble toxins continue to increase until the system backs up so badly that liver stones and gallstones form.

A leaky gut can result in the absorption of larger particles from your food across the intestine. You begin absorbing polypeptides rather than broken down amino acids. Your body sees the polypeptides as foreign and sets up an immune response, causing you to develop IgG food sensitivities.

The food sensitivities cause inflammation associated with migraines, ear infections, sinusitis, asthma, ADD, arthritis, etc. They aggravate virtually every inflammatory condition in the body. These conditions can affect all ages, even those who appear to be in excellent health.

Action step—IgG food sensitivities can be assessed with an ELISA test. Read *Dr. Braly's Food Allergy and Nutrition Revolution* by James Braly M.D.

It is regrettable that traditional medicine has almost completely ignored this functional cascade. As you can imagine, many drugs and surgeries aggravate this cascade of deteriorating health.

Even throughout the course of my medical training, I found my thinking was at odds with the traditional concept of healthcare. This was primarily because many therapeutic interventions dealt with symptomatic relief rather than correcting the underlying problem or condition. It was for this reason that after completing my undergraduate education I elected to apply to osteopathic medical training (DO) rather than allopathic training (MD). In the osteopathic training, we learned allopathic medicine, but we also learned structural medicine. With this structural training, I could actually heal many painful conditions directly by correcting misalignment of bones rather than relying on drugs and pain killers to cover symptoms. Over the years, I have learned that the more tools at my disposal the more precisely I can direct therapy. A patient may require surgery, physical therapy, prolotherapy, medications, or manipulative therapy. If I have all the tools, I can direct therapy to the patients' needs. As the old adage states, "If the only tool I have is a hammer, then everything begins to look like nails."

As I progressed through my medical training, I quickly found that symptomatic treatments were commonplace, and looking for underlying causal factors was often ignored.

Arthritis is an example. How often do doctors treat with non-steroidal anti-inflammatory medications? That is the treatment we were taught. How can it be wrong? It is wrong because such treatment ignores possible underlying factors such as bacterial infections, parasites, nutritional deficiencies, toxic exposures, free radical pathology, and more. The treatment with NSAIDS may be quick, easy, and accepted, but it can actually cause "leaky gut," which, in itself, leads to degenerative diseases such as arthritis. The arthritic condition can become worse because you used a NSAID to treat the symptoms. The treatment can make you feel better today, but your condition is worse next month because you used the therapy.

Another example is cholesterol. The number one prescribed medications are "statin" drugs to lower cholesterol…allegedly to decrease cardiovascular disease. This thought came about in the late '70s and early '80s after the Framingham study concluded that with proper weight control, diet, and exercise a person can lower the total cholesterol and raise the HDL (good cholesterol). This was shown to reduce hardening of the arteries. Drug companies quickly mobilized to find chemicals that would artificially lower cholesterol and raise HDL. Soon, "statin" drugs came on the scene…*and* with great marketing!

The truth is, though, that as of the writing of this book, there is little evidence demonstrating that by artificially lowering the cholesterol with these medications, the hardening of the arteries was reduced. Yet, due to the marketing, almost every doctor in the country will swear that "statin" drugs do exactly that.

I like to use an example. If one of your children were to get an "F" on their report card and, on the way home from school, they took a pen and changed the "F" to a "B," did that improve their performance in school? Of course not! Now they have to suffer the consequences of their poor performance in school *and* the repercussions of their actions.

A study out of Canada confirmed what I have been telling patients for years. Because "statin" drugs drain the body of a nutrient co-factor called "Co Q 10," the use of these medications can be linked to congestive heart failure and dementia. Co Q 10 is a nutrient essential to the Krebs energy cycle of the body. It is key to the production of energy especially in high oxygen areas such as the heart and brain! Depriving energy to these vital areas can result in congestive heart failure and dementia.

It is important to note that "statin" drugs have been shown to minimize the rupturing of vulnerable plaques. There are, though, less costly, natural enzymes that reduce the rupturing of vulnerable plaques without the side effects. The enzymes most frequently used to minimize the inflammation in blood vessels are those found in wobenzyme, which has been used for years in Europe for this very purpose.

There are also other means of lowering cholesterol without the consequences associated with using "statin" drugs. One example is a natural product called polycosanol. Polycosanol compares favorably with the "statin" drugs without the side effects.

Certainly weight control, diet, and exercise are key to good cardiovascular health!

Another logical approach to maintaining lower cholesterol levels and helping to detoxify are with natural substances containing plant sterols. These substances work in the intestine by binding to cholesterol and fat soluble toxins that have been dumped by the liver into the small intestine. By binding to these substances, it prevents the enterohepatic reabsorption and recycling of cholesterol and toxic materials back into the body. Thus, you detoxify, unplug, and decongest the liver and gallbladder and lower cholesterol at the same time. That's what I call functional medicine!

Our current obsession with lowering cholesterol may have another deleterious side-effect. Exposure to sunlight naturally converts cholesterol to vitamin D. The artificial lowering of cholesterol could be the cause of much of the vitamin D deficiency experienced by many patients taking cholesterol lowering medications. Vitamin D deficiency is implicated in heart disease, chronic pain, fibromyalgia, hypertension, arthritis, depression, inflammatory bowel disease, obesity, PMS, crohn's disease, cancer, MS, and other autoimmune diseases. The vitamin D council states that vitamin D deficiency can also cause strokes, osteoporosis, muscle weakness, muscle wasting, and birth defects.

Vitamin D also stimulates the immune system to naturally protect against colds and flu.

As a disclaimer, I am not against all drugs and surgery. As a physician, I write prescription drugs when necessary. I refer people for surgery when necessary. Much of this can be avoided, however, if we focus on the functional medicine paradigm addressed by this book. To learn more about these and other functional medicine concepts please visit our website: www.ihcenter.net.

There are myriads of variations on these and other general functional medicine paradigms. Therefore, it is important to find a physician trained in assessing and treating you from a functional, integrative approach.

Action step—You may find a doctor in your area that is practicing this type of functional (integrative) medicine by going on the web to International College of Integrative Medicine, American College of Advancement in Medicine, American College of Environmental Medicine, Functional Medicine Institute, and A4M.

Worldly Influences on Health and Healing

Dependence on Prescription Drugs
On April 15, 1998, the Palm Beach Post noted a study confirming how dangerous prescription drugs really are. They concluded that drug side effects make two million people sick each year, and that properly prescribed medicine kills 106,000 people each year. These statistics make drug side effects at least the forth most common cause of death in this country. The analysis, the largest and most complete of its kind, concludes that one in fifteen hospital patients in the United States can expect a serious reaction to prescription or even over-the-counter medicine. Approximately 5 percent of these will die from it. If the findings are accurate, then the number of people dying each year from drug

side effects may be exceeded only by the numbers of people dying from heart disease, strokes, and cancer. The evidence in this study is especially powerful because it looks only at cases in which the drugs were taken correctly.

The bigger picture is even more concerning, though. Virtually every prescription tells you to avoid using that particular prescription in combination with other medications because of possible adverse drug interactions. Yet almost every medication along with literally thousands of other potentially toxic chemicals are finding their way into our ecosphere—our water, our food, and the air we breathe. Such contamination is a ticking time bomb relative to our health. Therefore, whenever possible, avoid drugs. Our society has coddled the drug industry to the point that they are the sacred cow. We treat people as if they are stupid and subject them to chemical treatments that are dangerous and extremely costly. Drugs cause death. They often have serious effects…especially when taken with other drugs (chemicals). Many of these combinations of chemicals have never been tested. Alone, many chemicals have addictive potential and dependency issues. Is the risk/benefit ratio justified? Is the cost/benefit justified? When we mix these chemicals together is the experiment justified?

Medical Theory—
Germ Theory versus Biological Terrain

For centuries an argument has persisted between two schools of thought. The germ theory of medicine is based on "monomorphism" which means 'one form'. This theory can be traced back to brilliant scientists including Pliny, Linnaeus, Pasteur, and Koch.

In order to accept that a specific micro-organism is productive of disease,

1. it must be found in all cases of the disease,

2. it must be isolated from the host and grown in pure culture,

3. it must reproduce the original disease when introduced into a susceptible host, and

4. it must be found present in the experimental host so infected.[10]

The germ theory believes that germs are the cause of certain diseases such as chicken pox, mumps, measles, etc. These minute living micro-organisms are active and give off poisonous materials that destroy the tissues, the glands, and the organs of the body. When a person is ill, these germs are continually discharged in the waste of the body, such as urine, sweat, and fecal material.

The germ theory holds that germs are the enemy that should be killed by medicines. When one is sick or dying, this may be the appropriate approach. However, unless steps are taken to prevent re-infection, the problem can occur again.

In contrast, "pleomorphism" means "many forms." The expressed form is dependent on the biological terrain. The roots of this theory date back approximately two centuries to Almquist, Bergstrand, Enderlein, Bechamp, an adversary of Pasteur, and others. In more recent years, supporters of the terrain theory include Gaston Naessens, Robert Young, and Royal Rife.

This theory holds that germs start out in the body as small forms referred to as microzyma, somatids, and protists. These protists can change into bacterias, viruses, fungus, and back to their original form. Dr. Dennis Myers postulates that they go into a sixteen-stage cycle. These changed forms produce waste, which is actually the cause of pain, sickness, and disease in the body.

By purifying the blood, we can rebalance the system and fight the protists. But once the body is weakened by abusing it with alcohol, tobacco, improper food, over-eating, wrong food-combining, lack of exercise/sleep, overwork, and negative thinking, the body's pH is appropriate for the planting of the germs of disease.

An example in nature is how in the northern hemisphere moss grows only on the north side of the trees. The sun's ultraviolet rays cannot reach this area of the tree. In general, there is more moisture here. The environment is condusive to moss growing. The same concept is true within our bodies.

There is a significant difference in philosophy between the germ theory and the pleomorphic terrain theory of medicine. Therefore, the treatment approach is vastly different. It is interesting to note that Louis Pasteur was claimed to have stated on his death bed that Bechamp was right. "It is not the germ that causes disease but the terrain in which the germ was found."[11]

In the last century, the germ theory dominated the medical model because antibiotics saved many lives and the system is designed for drug companies to make huge profits that drive research, education, and politics. Now we have drugs that deal with virtually any sign or symptom imaginable. We have a fast food society that cannot wait to deal with underlying health issues directly. We want to feel good *now*. Drugs are the answer.

Obviously, some of what we are calling "functional medicine" coincides with the terrain theory. I have been confronted with arrogant doctors that claim they currently perform "evidence-based medicine," not the quackery I expound. I quickly point out that what I practice is evidence-based medicine in that it is based on sound, proven, scientific principles. It is based on biochemisty, anatomy, physiology, pathology, and pharmacology. The majority of doctors have been trained by the drug companies that sponsor seminars teaching doctors that medical care is treating disease symptoms with medication. The drug companies lead physicians to believe that everything is tested and reasonably safe. Yet how often do we hear of the pharmaceutical companies covering up information, and we soon discover that people are injured by the medications? To believe that traditional medicine is "evidence based" is incredibly short-sighted and hypocritical. How many studies have been done that evaluate the toxic effects incurred by a patient taking more than one medication at a time, let alone six, eight, or ten medications? Very few. Traditional medicine is a failing experiment. The cost in terms of lives destroyed, and dollars spent is astronomical. Therefore, if we can decrease toxic exposure by minimizing the use of medications, we are bound to win both physically and financially.

Numerous studies demonstrate that toxic exposures and the inability to adequately rid the body of its toxic load causes acidity in body tissues. Body acidity is associated with an environment primed to develop degenerative diseases. Even cancer thrives in an acidic environment. Therefore, detoxification is fundamental to maintaining health and well being.

As I stated earlier, in the last century, the germ theory dominated the medical model. That model has contributed to modifying the biological terrains within our bodies in a very negative way. We are becoming toxic and acidic. Our bodies are increasingly being attacked by free radicals from our environment. This contributes to the sky rocketing incidence of degenerative diseases and cancers.

To reverse this trend, we must focus on the biological terrain. Health and healing are found in modifying the terrain with our lifestyle choices and in eliminating all but essential drug and chemical exposures.

Chemicals and Disease

In the last century, the germ theory dominated. I believe that science is pushing free radical pathology as the new frontier we must conquer. Literally thousands of books, articles, and films confirm that our biosphere has been dramatically disturbed and chemically changed by human activities. According to (cf:Nocole MR 2002,ISP,College of Lifelong Learning; Wayne State University) in 1989 alone, more than one billion pounds of chemicals were released into the ground. These chemicals contaminate farm land and drinking water. Over 188,000,000 pounds of chemicals were also discharged directly into lakes and rivers. More than 2,400,000,000 pounds of chemicals were discharged into the air we breathe. In just one year, at least 5,705,670,380 pounds of chemical pollutants were released into our biosphere. We eat, breathe, and live in that environment!

All of these chemicals are toxic to some degree. They all generate free radicals that can cause free radical damage to our bodies. In a simplistic sense, free radicals are like sparks that attack our bodies contributing to aging, degenerative disease, cancer, etc. In some instances, the chemicals are similar to the natural biomolecules found in our body. They are mistakenly utilized in metabolic reactions and thus produce toxic metabolites causing disease. These processes can damage cell membranes as well as genetic molecules. Damage of genetic molecules can cause developmental defects. An example of this is demonstrated in the fact that a large amount of pesticides and fertilizers used on gardens, lawns, golf courses, etc. end up in ponds and lakes. Perhaps this is why we are finding so many frogs with deformities and developmental defects compared to forty or fifty years ago.

According to (Florence TM, Centre for Environmental and Health Science Pty Ltd, Sydney, NSW, Aust N Z J Opthalmal 1995; 23(1) Feb: 3-7), significant evidence has accumulated over the past three decades that most of the degenerative diseases have their origin in free radical pathology. These degenerative diseases include asthma, diabetes, dementia, atherosclerosis, cancer, inflammatory joint disease, degenerative eye disease, and more!

Antioxidants are used to combat free radicals. Some epidemiological studies suggest that since free radicals are involved in carcinogenesis then antioxidants may reduce cancer risk. Some survivors and clinicians have concluded that antioxidants are effective in preventing cancer reoccurrence. [12] Many oncologists discourage patients from taking antioxidants, though. They claim that the antioxidants interfere with chemo drugs and radiation therapy. The thought is that chemo-drugs and radiation generate large amounts of free radicals that kill cancer cells (along with normal healthy cells). Again, since the antioxidants scavenge the free radicals they might interfere with therapy. The bottom line is that despite the fact that research shows that free radicals are involved in carcinogenesis, the oncologists treat patients with chemotherapy and radiation that work by causing more free radicals!

A more logical approach to at least integrate into cancer therapy is insulin potentiation therapy. As mentioned earlier, cancer loves sugar. One of the differences between cancer cells and regular, healthy cells is that the cancer cell provides much less energy per molecule of sugar transported into the cell. For this reason, cancer cells protect themselves by having many more insulin receptors than do regular, healthy cells. In a simplistic sense, then, when low-dose insulin is administered, it selectively prepares the cancer cells for feeding. The chemotherapy agent is administered in a much lower concentration because it will selectively go to the cancer cells.

To understand how real this problem is, The Washington Post's (Tuesday, February 15, 2005; page HE01) Jim Morris reported that the US Federal Government issued an unusually detailed alert to the nation's 5.5 million health care workers.[13] The powerful drugs used in chemotherapy can themselves cause cancer and poss a risk to nurses, pharmacists, and others who handle them. Thomas Connor, a research biologist with the national Institute for Occupational Safety and Health (NIOSH), stated that chemotherapy drugs in human and animal studies have shown they have the potential to cause cancer or reproductive problems.

Over the last century, the incidence of breast cancer has risen greatly, and the sperm count in males has significantly declined. These phenomena coincide with the increased use of chemicals in industry and medicine. In areas of the body where there are rapidly dividing cells, as in the testicles for the production of sperm and where there is fatty tissue, there is a higher risk of developing disease states. Toxic chemicals are known to interfere with cell division and bio-accumulate in fatty tissue. They also generate free radicals that rob electrons from hormones.

It is not surprising that in the report "Male Reproductive Health Disorders and the Potential Role of Exposure to Environmental Chemicals" by Professor Richard Sharpe of the Medical Research Council (MRC) in Edinburgh, UK, it is revealed that many everyday chemicals have the potential to block the action of testosterone.[14] A baby's exposure to mixtures of these chemicals may harm future reproductive health. It may also cause birth defects, low sperm counts, and testicular cancer.

The incidence of cancer cannot be minimized. Currently the risk of a man developing cancer is nearly 1 in 2. The risk of a woman developing cancer in her lifetime is nearly 1 in 3.[15] Cancer death rates have nearly tripled since 1900. According to the American Cancer Society 41,000 Americans (64 people per 100,000) died of cancer in 1900. According to the Center of Disease Control and Prevention (CDC) "In 2005, an estimated 570,280 Americans-more than 1500 people a day will die of cancer. (nearly 200 people per 100,000).[16]

The Collaboration of Health and the Environment (CE database report links chemical contaminants with 180 disease conditions, ranging from skin rashes to fertility issues to cancer.[17] These problems are further aggravated as we try treating symptoms caused by chemicals with other toxic chemicals we call drugs that are prescribed as "medications."

It is my opinion that we need to legislate the clean up of the environment. We, as humans, cannot continue to inundate ourselves with environmental toxins. We must also detoxify ourselves.

Much of the most toxic substances we deal with cause the accumulation of heavy metals in our bodies. Heavy metals bind to our tissues, block normal metabolic pathways, and produce an abundance of free radicals. Again, these free radicals cause aging, degenerative diseases and cancer.

There are a variety of ways to remove such heavy metals from the tissues. In mild conditions, ingesting nutrients like alpha lipoic acid and pectins may help. In other conditions garlic, cilantro, and/or chlorophyll may help. Many conditions require the use of chelating agents such as EDTA, DMSA, and DMPS. These chelating agents also act as "anionic surfactants" that aggressively neutralize free radicals.

Action step—If you suspect that heavy metals may be contributing to your health problems, contact ACAM (American College for the Advancement of Medicine) or ICIM (International College of Integrative Medicine) to find a doctor with the training to treat you properly.

A general resource to learn more about functional medicine is our website: www.integrativehealthcarecenter.net. The above are also resources to learn more about functional integrative medicine. If you are a physician, you can receive training from the organizations listed above.

AAL
1715 E Wilshire Ste 715
Santa Ana, CA 92705
800-522-2611
Antioxidant test #450

ALLETESS
216 Pleasant Street
Rockland, MA 02370
Elisa IgG Food Allergies
Mold Panel IgE and IgG
H. Pylori
Food Sensitivity and Allergy

DOCTORS DATA
3755 Illinois Ave
Chicago, IL 60185
800-323-2784
Metals Hair Analysis
Comprehensive Stool Analysis
Fecal and Urine Metals Analysis

GREAT SMOKIES (GENOVA)
63 Zillicoa Street
Ashville, NC 28801
800-522-4762
Adrenal Cortex Stress
Amino Acids Plasma
Comprehensive Stool Analysis
Fatty Acids

Female Hormone Profile (saliva and blood serum)
Male Hormone Profile
Genomics

IMMUNO LABS
6801 Powerline Road
Fort Lauderdale, FL 33309
800-231-9097
Eliza IgG Foods
Candida Albicans Assay

METAMETRIX
4855 Peachtree Ind Blvd #201
Norcross, GA 30092
800-221-4640
Amino Acid 40
Fatty Acid Plasma

SPECTRACELL
10401 Town Park Drive
Houston, TX 77072
800-227-5227
Micronutrient Testing

The Web of Functional Health

We have learned that health starts with God—His power and His energy. If we choose to let Christ shine through us, His energy manifests in the fruits of the Tree of Life. Those fruits will stimulate healing endorphins and further energize our world in a positive way. If we then nourish our bodies with clean air and clean water, as well as balanced amino acids, fatty acids, vitamins and minerals, we have a strong foundation for health and positive genetic expression.

We must focus on eliminating parasites, toxic metals, and chemicals that pollute our bodies and interfere with healthy function. Just like we need to change the oil and filters in our cars, we need to keep our bodies clean inside and out to maximize health. Detoxification through fasting, saunas, colonics, chelation, treating leaky gut, etc. goes a long way toward this goal. Then, following the analogy of an automobile, we must get our exercise to stay "tuned up." Just like they say about cars, you need to run them a bit to burn the gunk out.

The Web of Functional Health

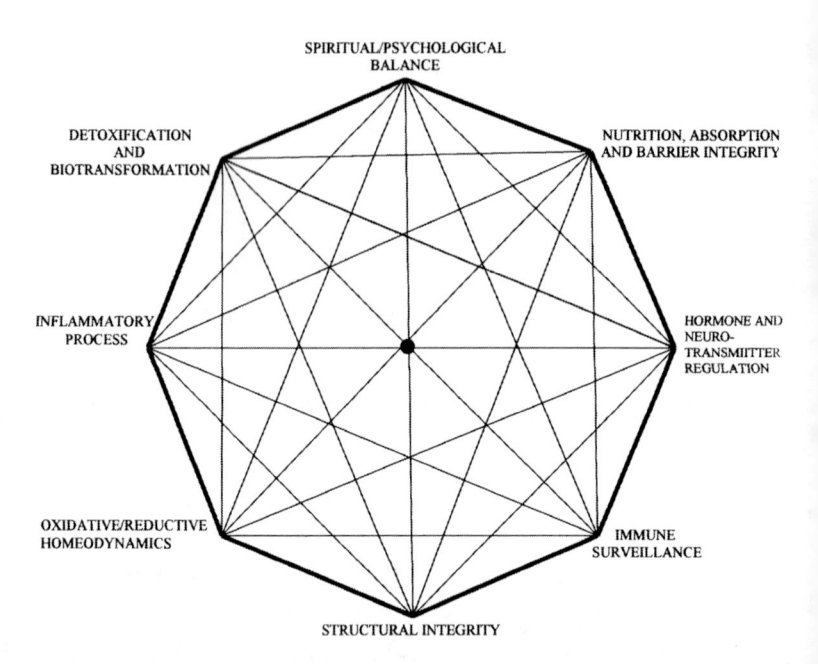

- SPIRITUAL/PSYCHOLOGICAL BALANCE
- NUTRITION, ABSORPTION AND BARRIER INTEGRITY
- HORMONE AND NEUROTRANSMITTER REGULATION
- IMMUNE SURVEILLANCE
- STRUCTURAL INTEGRITY
- OXIDATIVE/REDUCTIVE HOMEODYNAMICS
- INFLAMMATORY PROCESS
- DETOXIFICATION AND BIOTRANSFORMATION

As you can see by the diagram, healthy bodily function is a multifaceted balance. The spiritual/psychological balance relates to the effects of the spirit on the soul and how this affects our health. Detoxification and biotransformation relates to how we handle the toxins and chemicals we are exposed to. Inflammation is a byproduct of toxic/chemical exposures, candida, leaky gut, food sensitivities, etc. Oxidative/reductive homeodynamics relate to the balance of free radicals and antioxidants. Imbalance results in oxidative stress. Oxidative stress results in more rapid aging, degenerative diseases, and the development of cancer. Nutrition, absorption, and barrier integrity relate to food choices, supplement choices, and the assimilation of those important, nutritional components. Hormone and neurotransmitter regulation can be measured and regulated naturally and safely. Structural integrity affects proper function of nerves and energy flow within the body. It is also key to normal organ and glandular function. It is integral in maintaining balance and minimizing pain throughout the body. Finally, when all of these are in balance, our immune system will function better, and health is maximized.

Strive to be functionally centered. If imbalance persists, consider each of these factors from the diagram. Any of these, if imbalanced, can lead to disease.

God Bless.

Practical Advice for Living a Long, Healthy Life

According to the book *The Blue Zones* by Dan Buettner, there are lifestyle characteristics common to populations of people that live longer and healthier than most. The following characteristics are condensed from that book and from my medical studies.

The Basics

- Always do your best and always do the right thing.

- Live a lifestyle of moderation and enjoy life's simple pleasures. Be thankful.

- Do not smoke. Avoid second hand smoke and other toxins (including drugs whenever possible).

- Maintain a healthy body mass index (BMI).

- Detoxify with such things as saunas, chelation, antioxidants, fasting, etc.

- Get out into the sun ten to fifteen minutes at least twice weekly.

- Cultivate a positive attitude. Confess positives and surround yourself with positive people.

- Have a purpose in life—a reason to get up each day.

- Belly laugh—laugh with friends.

- Work on and maintain friendships.

- Establish sanctuaries of time like the Sabbath to focus on God, family, nature, and camaraderie.

- De-stress your life.

- Reduce the noise in your life. Consider meditation or yoga. I recommend setting aside quiet time with God.

- Plant a garden.

- Work hard and get your body physically tired.

- Get seven to nine hours of sleep each night.

Eating Habits and General Nutritional Advise

A. Avoid processed food, trans-fats, and excess sugar.

B. Eat lean cuts of meat, cis-fats, and low glycemic index carbohydrates.

C. Ingest moderate amounts of flavanoids found in such things as red wine, brightly colored fruits, vegetables, and dark chocolate.

D. Eat a lean plant-based diet accented with meat.

E. Drink goat's milk.

F. Eat sweet potatoes.

G. Eat some soy.

H. Eat nuts.

I. Eat apples.

J. Eat oranges.

K. Avoid pork.

L. Drink plenty of water.

M. Eat breakfast like a king, lunch like a prince, and dinner like a beggar.

N. Always eat in moderation. (Moderate servings.)

O. Make snacking a hassle. Buy smaller packages of food. Eat slowly. Focus on the food and not on other things like the television.

P. Weigh yourself daily.

Personality Issues

A. Don't compare yourself to others…you don't know what their journey is all about.

B. Don't have negative thoughts…especially about things you can't control. Invest yourself in the positives of the present moment.

C. Do not overdue…set limits.

D. Don't take yourself too seriously. No one else does.

E. Don't gossip.

F. Dream more while you are awake.

G. Envy is a waste of time.

H. Forget the past and focus on your present happiness. Remember, no one is responsible for your happiness except for you.

I. Don't hate people.

J. Forgive everyone.

K. Realize that life is a school. You are here to learn. Each problem is simply a part of your curriculum. The lessons learned, not the problems, are what is important.

L. You don't have to win every argument. Agree to disagree. Calm explanations and discussions are nice.

M. Treat others as you want to be treated.

N. Don't make jokes at the expense of others.

Your Support Structure

A. Formulate a purpose for your life.

B. Look for others who share your life's purpose.

C. Continue learning new things.

D. Be early to appointments.

E. Get involved. Go and do things. Go to church.

F. Explore new traditions for yourself, your family, and your friends.

G. Live in a smaller house to get closer to your family members, if you can.

H. Celebrate elders.

I. Be likable.

J. Identify an inner circle of supportive friends and relatives.

K. Spend time each day interacting with your inner circle.

L. Spend time with like minded friends.

M. Give back…volunteer and help others.

Action step——I encourage you to read the book *The Blue Zones* by Dan Buettner. And remember…Knowledge is knowing what to do…Wisdom is doing it!

Crossing Over

Key to health—Focus on life.

"Some women received again their dead by resurrection. Others were tortured to death with clubs, refusing to accept release (offered on the terms of denying their faith), that they might be resurrected to a better life" (Hebrew 11:35, AMP).

"But I am hard pressed between the two. My yearning desire is to depart-to be free of this world, to set forth-and be with Christ, for that is far, far better" (Phillipians 1:23, AMP).

Keys to the Kingdom

"Therefore pray in this manner: Our Father in Heaven, hallowed be thy name. Thy Kingdom come.

Thy will be done, as in Heaven so on earth. Give us bread for our needs from day to day. And forgive us our offenses, as we have forgiven our offenders. And do not let us enter into temptation, but deliver us from evil. For Thine is the Kingdom and the Power and the Glory for ever and ever" Matthew 6:9-13, Lamsa).

In this book, we have established "Keys to Health" from God's Word. Those keys relate to tapping into God's kingdom on earth. It is worth reiterating those keys:

1. Accept the fact that you are forgiven in Christ, and God considers you worthy (John 3:16, Lamsa).

2. You must believe. You must have faith in God (Mark 6:2-6, Lamsa).

3. Don't blame God for what Satan does. Satan is the author of sickness and disease (John 10:10 and Acts 10:38, Lamsa).

4. Know that your body is the temple of the Holy Spirit and treat it as such (1 Corinthians 6:19, 20, Lamsa).

5. Seek Godly wisdom (James 3:13-18, Lamsa).

6. Stay rooted in Jesus Christ (Mark 4:17, Lamsa).

7. Have no fear of this world…trust God (Job 3:25, Lamsa).

8. Fear and worship God (Proverbs 3:7, 8 and 10:27, Lamsa).

9. Serve the Lord Jesus Christ (Exodus 23:25, 26 and Hebrews 8:6, Lamsa).

10. Love (agape) (1 Corinthians 13:1-13, NKJV).

11. Do not be double-minded (James 1:5-8, Lamsa).

12. Honor your parents (Ephesians 6:1-3, Lamsa).

13. Obey God's Commandments, not the doctrines of men (Mark 7:6-13, Lamsa).

14. Properly discern the Lord's body—communion (1 Corinthians 11:27-32, Lamsa).

15. Have a happy heart (Proverbs 17:22, Lamsa).

16. Forgive (Mark 11:25, 26, Lamsa).

17. Always speak positive words (Proverbs 18:20, 21, Mark 11:23, 24, and Numbers 14:27, 28, Lamsa).

18. Know and understand God's Word (Hosea 4:6, Lamsa).

19. Focus on God, not the cares of this life (Mark 4:19, Lamsa).

20. Do not regard iniquity in your heart (Psalms 66:18, AMP).

21. Remember God's benefits (Psalms 103:2-5, Lamsa).

22. Obey the voice of God (Exodus 15:26, Ezekiel 33:11, Lamsa).

23. Have faith and do not give up (Galatians 6:9, Hebrews 6:12, Hebrews 10:35, 36, Lamsa).

24. Focus on life (Hebrews 11:35 and Philippians 1:23, Lamsa).

A Thought for the Terminally Ill

An ill patient confided in his doctor, "I am afraid to die. What is on the other side?"

The doctor quietly responded, "I don't know."

The ill patient continued, "You are a Christian doctor, and you don't know what is on the other side?"

Suddenly, the sound of scratching and whining was heard outside of the exam room. The doctor opened the door to the exam room, and his dog jumped up into his arms. The doctor turned back to the ill patient and said, "My dog has never been in my office before. He didn't know what was on the other side of this door. All he knew was that his master was here. When the door opened, he jumped in without fear. In the same way, I know little of what is on the other side of death, but be assured that your master is there, so have no fear.

Last Thoughts

Now that you have read *Revelations in a Brown Paper Bag*, you may be thinking it strange that I choose a God-centered, in-Christ approach to health and healing. It is because that is what I know. I have been miraculously healed with prayer myself. If you have another God that can do the same thing…then ask him.

If, though, there is no reply, remember that Jesus is waiting patiently and lovingly for you to accept Him into your heart. He loves you. He died for you, too. Put Him at the center of your life, and you can live the abundant life filled with God's blessings. You, too, can be healed!

You might argue that you have not been called to faith in Christ. Salvation simply was not preordained. "If I do not accept Christ as my Savior then it simply was not God's will for me to be saved." To answer this, please consider the following example.

A business owner needed help, so he placed a help wanted ad. Some answered. They heard the terms. Some accepted and some rejected employment. The business took the responsibility for offering the job and for the hiring. Those hired also took responsibility for being hired because they responded to the help wanted ad and accepted the terms of employment.

The fact that you are reading this now, you can no longer say that God did not place His "Help Wanted" ad in front of you. He has offered you eternal life. Please respond with "Yes, Jesus, come into my heart." Repent and accept His forgiveness. He loves you and wants to fellowship with you now and forever!

By doing this simple act of faith, scripture says you become crucified with Christ. Nevertheless, you live, but it is not you. It is Christ living in you. As the Lord works in your life, you will be transformed. You will find that your desires will change. You will find yourself not wanting so much to please your flesh. The flesh is crucified. Your desires will be to please God. Then, when you cross over, you can expect to hear, "Well done good and faithful servant. Come on in!"

Endnotes

1. "Christ Has No Hands But Ours", http://pitter/epostings.blogspot.com/2009/12/christ-has-no-hands-but-ours.html, last modified 12/11/11

2. Rutz, James. Mega Shift. Colorado Springs: Empowerment Press, 2005

3. The Constitution of Liberty, The Definitive Edition, Ronald Hamowy, ed., v.17, The collected works of F.A. Hayek, University of ChicagoPress

4. Henry W. Wright, A More Excellent Way, A division of Pleasant Valley Church Inc. Thomaston, Georgia 30286, Seventh Edition, copyright 2005 Pleasant Valley Church, Inc.

5   "Mother Teresa Prayer", http://www.inspriation-oasis.com/mother-teresa-prayer.html, last modified 1/1/2012

6   Mandelbaum, Allen, trans. The Divine Comedy of Dante Alighieri Inferno. Berkley: University of California Press, 1982

7   Mandelbaum, Allen, trans. The Divine Comedy of Dante Alighieri Inferno, Berkley: University of California Press, 1982

8   "Zoe-Life", http://www.wordbasedcounseling.org/Articles/Zoe-Life.htm., last modified 12/8/11

9   Breasted, James Henry, "The Edwin Smith Surgical Papyrus: published in facsimile and hieroglyphic transliteration with translation and commentary in two volumes". University of Chicago Oriental Institute Publications, v.3-4 Chicagop: University of Chicago Press, 1991

10 Koch's Postulates, dictionary.com, Merriam-Webster's Medical Dictionary, Merriam-Webster, Inc., http://dictionary.references.com/browse/koch'spostulates (accessed, 01/08/12)

11 "Biological Terrain vs. The Germ Theory", http://timelessremedies.wordpress.com/2007/10/29/biological-terrain-vs-the-germ-theory/

12 Jean et al, "Nutrition During and After Cancer Treatment: A Guide* for Informed Choices by Cancer Survivors," CA Cancer J. Clin51 (2001):153-181.

13 Jim Morris, The Washington Post, February 15, 2005, HE01.

14 "Male Reproductive Health Disorders and the Potential Role of Exposure to Environmental Chemicals", Accessed 12/12/11, http://www.env-health.org/spip.php?article829

15 Lifetime Probability of Developing or Dying From Cancer", http://www.cancer.org/Cancer/CancerBasics/lifetime-probability-of-developing-or-dying-from-cancer, last modified 12/10/11

16 "Cancer-A Modern Day Scourge",http://ezinearticles.com/?cancer-A-Modern-Day-Scourge&id=103970, last modified 12/9/11.

17 "The Collaboration of Health and the Environment", http://healthandenvironment.org/tddb/ , Accessed 12/11/11